A PART OF TRUTH

Collected Poems

by

W J Duff

Edited with an Introduction by
Roger Morsley Smith

The Gatesden Press
4 Pumping Station Road
Chiswick
LONDON W4 2SN

Published by
The Gatesden Press
4 Pumping Station Road
Chiswick
LONDON W4 2SN

ISBN 978-0-9554896-0-0

First Published 2007

The Gatesden Press
4 Pumping Station Road
Chiswick
LONDON W4 2SN

Printed by Wellington Press Group, London.

To Nancy

CONTENTS

INTRODUCTION

The poems in this book tell the story of one man's endeavour, which lasted a lifetime, to shed light on the human condition:

> "A part of truth that would not be
> Save by his touch and heed,
> Whose music only thrusts to life
> Through him, as through a reed."

To discover why much of this work is only published now, though written decades earlier, we must look back to 1970, when a strange, unwieldy organisation called NAMMA was forming in Munich, Germany. This novel conglomerate had an important task: the procurement of Tornado aircraft. Separate parts of the plane were to be designed and manufactured in Britain, Germany and Italy and the controlling NATO agency, NAMMA, staffed by officials from these countries, was a polyglot hybrid with severe functional difficulties. It was also quite an adventurous posting, for the project might be cancelled early on.

As a young civil servant, struggling to find my feet in this hectic melée, I consulted the files, to find them inadequate and crammed with verbiage. But as I read and discarded, questioned and sighed, I noticed writing of striking clarity, by someone who knew what he was doing: reserved, spare even, but with touches of dry humour. I prized these stepping stones through the morass and sought out the author, W J Duff, thus beginning a long friendship. Bill was no stranger to Germany; his mother was of German origin and he spoke German well. His wife, Nancy, had a first class honours degree and taught German; their son Matthew was similarly talented.

Like many of his generation, Bill Duff never knew his father, who was killed at the Battle of the Somme shortly before the boy's birth on 13 December 1917. Bill was simply brought up in Horsham by an aunt and uncle (the gardener in one poem). Perhaps the removal of a generation of talent stimulated the regard of many thoughtful youngsters in the 1930s for learning, literature, politics and discussion. Bill shared this quality; moreover he was clever. At Collyer's School his talent in English was encouraged by Joe Brearley, the teacher later revered by Harold Pinter. Bill gained a State Scholarship (that hallmark of brilliance) but for financial reasons entered the Civil Service, remaining there until retirement in 1982. This period was interrupted twice: during World War II, he served in Africa, Italy and Austria with 16/5 Lancers, 1942-1946 and in 1970-1973 he worked in NAMMA.

Munich was the flowering of Bill's career. A modest, diffident man, the excellence of his work was at last fully recognised, for effective staff in NAMMA influenced progress far more than their normal responsibilities would have allowed. Bill was reticent, shy even, yet sure of his worth. A tall, big-built, somewhat angular man with sparse hair, horn rimmed spectacles and clothes untouched by fashion, kindly and gentle, he shunned the limelight. I liked to hear his slow, gravelly voice explaining a complex question, breaking off to smile or joke occasionally, for humour was integral to him. He possessed a transparent integrity rare anywhere but particularly in NAMMA. Although he was a very private man, everyone cherished his company; his staff was devoted. We seldom met socially in Munich, however, for our ages and circumstances were very different.

On my return to the UK in 1974, I missed the country where I had perfected my German and come to feel at home. Once again I contacted Bill, who in some ways felt similarly, finding Britain tame and unsatisfying. He extended sympathy and hospitality at the family home in Leatherhead. One day, when I mentioned my attempts to write poetry, he shyly said he too dabbled in this pursuit, "a mug's game" as he wryly called it, though actually it was vital to his life. Late each night he sat at his desk, formulating, musing, puffing on his pipe. Nor did he restrict himself to the usual subjects; political satire, humour and translations were included. Poetry was his way of coming to terms with life. I was surprised by the high standard of his verse; all the more so to learn that it was largely unpublished.

Although poems appeared in The Poetry Review, Autumn 1962 and 1963; in The Pattern of Poetry 1963; in New Poems 1967 and in "Orbis" in 1986, novelty was then in vogue, not the established forms at which Bill excelled, and no publisher would take a comprehensive collection. After his death on 14 March 1988, Nancy published a selection, entitled "Curtain Calls" (Association of Little Presses). In view of its small circulation and the merit of the poems, most are republished now. As Nancy's preface rightly says: "Old-fashioned in style some may call his work but the thoughts on Love, Life and Death are as valid today as ever." Tastes in poetry have swung back somewhat, so this is even more true today.

In making this selection at the request of Bill and Nancy's daughter, Caroline, herself an accomplished scholar, I have had to choose from a very large number of poems. Some were too wordy, as the author himself recognised. The translations of Goethe have also been omitted. The poems are not in strict order of composition but do fall into a rough chronological sequence. Many celebrate events, such as wartime experience, separation, New Year's Eve, the death of a friend, a girl glimpsed in the street; perhaps a moment of inspired harmony with nature, a feeling at the core of Bill's beliefs:

> "The sense that past our grasping it is well,
> That rock and artefact and creature stand
> Each fitly on its plinth of being and all
> The bricks of time lie squarely in their place."

Despite his learning, Bill's images are homely and apt:

> "Philosophy's engendered in the heart,
> Not in the mind, and hunts shop windows for
> The arguments it needs....."

The shorter poems are attractive, being easy to read, and achieving more than many poets do on such occasions. However, it is in the long poems, "Conversation 1964," “Conversation 1975” and "Aneurism 1985", the last written after a serious illness, that Bill found his métier. Here is wisdom and humanity seldom encountered; an intellect levelled at the stars. Nobody can solve life's mystery, as Bill knew, but to try is a noble task. He also examines the art of poetry, which:

> Chooses with dice but will not be denied,
> At prayer or bidding neither comes nor stays"

He felt too the isolation of the poet, who toils alone; knowing that in the end he must follow Yeats:

"   ...driving like a prow
Through ebbing days, who steered his
                    battened freight
Into the darkness, scorning anchorage."

The question first asked in “Conversation 1964”:

> "What moved us, love or fear? Were we defeated?"

receives its answer, a consoling one, in "Aneurism 1985," for this is poetry of affirmation, not resignation or despair. Beauty pervades these poems, which acknowledge humanity's integral place in the universe. Bill followed no strict religion but had a deep spiritual quality. His was a:

"Faith picturing nothing, speech nor form
Nor even shadow cast;
Faith such as holds when faith is gone
And thought of it is past:
Sheer faith that some strange love and name
Will touch us at the last..."

I very much hope the poems will now reach a wider audience, who may be surprised to find their deepest thoughts - hitherto perhaps obscure - brought magically to light. This is no easy task, for:

"....truth has to be lived, since simple
Reason cannot win it;
And, as in Hamlet, there is pain
And error to begin it,
With no Euclidian chain to prove
There's all or nothing in:

And, as with Hamlet, there's no theme
Or overt moral shown
But planes and vistas that the heart
Had never guessed or known:
And truth can touch us in the end
By metaphors alone."

W J Duff sought truth, and found it more often than most men. One can only guess at the struggles his quest exacted, though the difficult terrain he traversed is apparent from "Conversation 1975:"

"And somehow is attained -
In part, ephemerally, unsurely - that
Ground beyond time and the opacities
Of which we had no thought; an absolute,
Balancing peace and tumult,
                                        glimpsed and then
Lost, and remembered only as a point
To be regained ..."

If through this book others are inspired to attempt a similar journey that would be sufficient for him.

Roger Morsley Smith
November 2006

ACKNOWLEDGEMENTS

Thanks are due to Christine Riley for reading the proofs, to Rachel Yih for typing and computer formatting and to Caroline Duff for support and understanding.

The Search - "Self's ultimate reason"

Evening

Through the trees, lights and a clock striking:
Slowly the evening drifts, slowly the hours.
One hemisphere is night with a shadow clinging,
A nature sleeping under a sky of flowers.

Come from the window, gentle-featured lady,
Come to the lamp and the talking by and by.
Turn from the trees, the dim nostalgic beauty,
And the stars which signal time across the sky.

The Match

Striking a match, on impulse he
Held it up -
Cigarette unlit -

And our eyes went to it;
And the small
Precocity of its blaze

Hushed us, like some miniature
Primal torch
Steadying in a cave;

Blue-based, nibbling at its shaft,
With black stalk
Filamenting the flame;

Tongue tasting the skin of dark -
Our one light,
Though this was full day:

It guttered then, self-fed, as if
An eye closed.
Our talk began again.

Beauty

By law, by law
Beauty dwells
On the stone's face,
Changes with flaw
And the year's blows.
Beauty alone
From prime goes
To new prime,
From grace to grace.
Forget all else,
Not this. Time
Hammers the stone.

Exile

If peace were to be sought,
It might be here. Cornflower and marigold
Wallow in light upon the crumbled earth,
Bold and prolific; poppy, geum, phlox
Lean from the shade to blossom: this red rose,
Standing in naked beauty, could pluck back
The paradisal thought.

And the small creatures still
Carry their simple attributes in patience
To the day's end and shoulder no intent
But to be creature - ant in solemn duty,
Ungainly bee, and fragile mouse that runs
From bush to bush; the pausing spider like
A brooch upon the sill.

Unheeded I look on,
Whose whim could summarily uproot or crush
Like storm or pounding rockfall, yet with no
God's power to touch and audit. Their regard
Turns inward to the stance and deed that bear
Type in fulfilment infinitely to ends
Finite and long since won.

All act their duty. I,
I stand in fallow, speculating on
The brilliance and utility of these,
That celebrate the sun, that spend themselves
To deck the hour, to burgeon and beget,
And faithfully each spring are minted new:
I was sent here to die -

To die, to die alone,
To die through many years, to die in lack
Of skills and fruitfulness, with no bequeathed
Language or hope, and no vocation save
The very dying. Under the spread leaves
I watch the shadows move and sense the hours
Endlessly overthrown.

Soon I shall reckon out
What's reckonable; but first I must rehearse
Probable griefs - for her death and for his,
For their indifference, for my own regret's
Conscienceless withering - so that I have ready
Words, consolations, talismans against
The loneliness and drought.

This shall be done; and then,
Then for mere pastime or out of my archaic
Habit of thought, to set the other down -
The sum of my unsubtle cogitation -
That is the only labour. When it's written,
I'll screw it up and toss it to the wind
And never think again.
Today I climbed upon
The humped back of the land, the path where once
So many walked and said 'How beautiful.'
The great cliff crumbles here and nothing sounds
But the sea's pulse. I met the kiss of air,
Touched the salt boulders and the humble grass,
Saw the wide waters run;

The blue salve of the sea -
Beginning, end; the sightless rollers marching;
Destruction without bitterness; the shining
Purity of the wave. I passed the chapel
In ruin on the shore, whose stone madonna
Robed in green sea-wrack stands and blindly gazes,
Unworshipped, solitary.

Has she no blessings more?
On the cold estuary through dipping buoys
The beaked ships move. The muffled crews steer on;
The cargoes are mere pretext - what they seek
Is trade with their own fear and loneliness,
The fleece of their imagined self, a final
Barter at the wind's core.

They search and shall not find.
Motion and distance, the sublime deceivers,
Shall hold their eyes and drain their purposes,
Perplex them utterly. When they return,
Their hearts so shall be wrought as if it were
This haven that they sailed for, this green
Landfall for which they pined.

Each blurs into the mist;
And I that chronicle stood on the hill
And watched them go. Then sadly I came down,
As evening reconnoitred, owning neither
Envy nor hope. All, all, it seemed, proceeded
Towards but falling short of consummation,
Ran on or came to rest,

Spelt itself out unbroken
In tireless iteration. Forms and colours
Slept for replenishment; and without break
Identities, acts, processes of time
In surf of images and with an ancient
Obstinacy crowded on the threshold of
A statement never spoken.

Heartstricken land, your face
Betrays no pain. Wounded, you heal. The seasons
Tread without respite, patiently restore
The appurtenances of that delight which shoots
But never bursts the bud. Breathe on outside,
Unsleeping in the dark. What deed you wished -
In time, in mood, in place -

That dying would not swerve,
What distillation of your devious will,
What ritual gift; I cannot answer this
Nor find your word, though nightly in all weathers
Here at this table with my book and pencil
I laboured in good faith. But leave it now:
The less than truth must serve.

God's Myth

It is God's myth. His thesis shall contain
The shipwrecked soul, the madman's pitiful eyes,
Malice and hunger. It has logic in
The ant labouring with a breadcrumb, the flies
Dancing and dying; it records
Movement of dust, a sleeper's indrawn breath
Soft in the lampless night, a single bird's
Shadow upon the waves, falling to death.

Eternal argument, exploding forever
On a pin's head of time! There is pain
Irrigating mercy; evil to discover
Faith in the heart's small cloister. There is our joy
In the crevices of His word. There is dismay,
Love and despair and loss; and love again.

Times in Time

So, you erupt again, compelling upon me the old
Delirium as of love. Bees totter out; the spider
Walks at your nod; rooks, brazen seed-gobblers,
Rig their shanty nests in the beech's bare scaffold.

Hares race the plough, chalk flinty furrows worn
And crumbled by the rain's heel, larks wrestling a wind
The violets crouch from: and everywhere times in time
Bud and peal out in leaf at the season's turn.

Times in my time, worlds in me folded, that declare
Nothing, but detonate, die for me - the guileless
Generations of sap and brilliance, flower-faces
Hanging your bright, blind innocence upon the air -

I wince at your reviving passion, this rude
Tumult's drum-roll crescendo, green days already striding
Towards self-forgotten fall, times dying in my pulse-time,
Counted only by the soft clock in my blood.

I shall see this again and record it: beyond the tall
Banners and password whisper of hope, the lusty
Regiment's utter defeat, the silence, the death without
anger
In crumpling fire. I foresee it, for all

Springs perish in me: I inhabit my own hour:
I carry the coiled hieroglyph, the datum, the unformulaed
Spinning of the word. Forgive me, pity me: I came
At other bidding and move beyond your power.

Homo Sapiens

Moralising beast, caretaker
Of this green estate, steward of the skull's
Ill-lit and draughty manor, it needs
No astrologies to read your doom.

Clearly you were blest: witness
Pity, ecstasy, all those
Deeds in the gust of morning:
Witness your old proclivities -

As, smitten, to kneel, claiming
All guilts into your stipend, from
His who at the first benison wept
To theirs, the yet unseeded;

And, on your small autonomy standing,
To proclaim love viable and carve it
On the rockface. So now proclaim it,
Here in midwinter: send your voice,

As the wind shouts and scathes and time
Lost on the great moor circles,
Gently into the darkness. Plead
For the arrogant and misbegotten.

Aberystwyth: View from the Hill

Climbers at daffodil-time, we pause to glance
Back at the houses grey as sediment
Dropped near the river's mouth, at naked green
Harpooned Pendinas floating like a whale.

Gull-high in silence hoisted, we observe
How, dark as tear-rinsed eyes, the sea at flow
Trades with the reef, and how the small capes point,
Wet-footed but defiant, to the west.

The town proceeds without us, like a play:
A train by Hornby puffs inland and whistles
Loud as a gnat; and millimetre men
Loiter or walk their inches out, while we

Gaze down like prophets from this rocky brow.
All who tread here are cleansed. See, at our feet,
A bird's pure skull, the emblem of a thought
Too sad or subtle for the lips to frame;
And through gigantic chambers of the air
Sun and high wind toil at their purposes.
The earth throws out strange shoots; the waves below
Tower and crumble; mews pass, sleeping on

The pallet of the gale. We go at length,
Turning for Clarach through the bleat of lambs,
Past cropped and crowded hills, the tardy year
Showing us simple celandines with some

Scatter of violets, small swerving rills
That surge and glint across the paths which fall
To Cwm woods scarce in bud. We pick our way
Over out-thrusting boulders, crack the twigs

Flung down by storms, fatigue or afterthought
Hushing our tongues. What wary self looks out
Caged in mortality, what waif of sense,
To savour still that visionary world,

Time's slow and simple death, begetting all -
The season' countermarch; the theme of bays
Recurring, fading; wingtilt over headlands;
Ystwyth to Rheidol at the sea's grave altar

Wed in one valley - all, all that derives
From the old prototype of grace and blooms
Without reproach, looks past our nervous blessing
And sinks back to its source to be regiven.

Water Rat

Remember the child's story, how
Water Rat, the shabby sullen loner,
A rat's rat in all else, had this one
Blinding, devastating skill - to carve
Delicate things from bone.

That ship he gave mutely to Grey Rabbit,
When she had done something terrifically
Decent for him - the filigree beauty of it!
Even Wise Owl's eyes bulged (Try saying that
Thirteen times quickly).

Miss Uttley (I respect her writing) observed
Without comment. The art gift, to her mind,
Had root, clearly, in rather doubtful soil.
That could be true: perhaps if you went back
Right to the start you'd find

That at one point the mooning inwardness
Of some prototype neurotic impressed
The competent boar-sticking oafs. They forsook
The development of spear-head technologies
To goggle as he placed

His hand upon the rock for a stencil
At Gargas. When at Pech Merle he sketched
Beast-figures on the wall and the hunt
Fortuitously flourished, there was a murmur.
At Willendorf next,

In a trough of the conception curve
He shaped a pregnant Venus. And then
Nothing could check him; lo, his seed prospered,
Dealing in priesthoods, acknowledged by
Credulous science-men.

Yet there is more to it, surely, the Water
Rat business, than that. Is it not
(If one rejects extra-mortal hypotheses)
Bred into the genus like Schadenfreude,
Schizophrenia and snot?

For it goes incorrigibly on and on,
Without measure or reason. My thought
Turns to an old rambler in a room,
Daubing behind locked doors, creating
As if for the sport

And scrapping the used canvasses after:
Another kneels in a draughty shed, chips -
Quite inexpertly, I am certain -
Towards a dream's core, from which his mind's
Purchase already slips.

Unbalanced? Well yes, if you can define
Any norm of equilibrium; but no
More so, surely, than their spectacular
Kindred - I mean the great block-busters,
Jack Milton & Co.

Failure is relative only; each lives by
The trick he has made up - e.g. musicians,
Deaf to finger-tapping impatience,
Swoon at their own cacophony. Most,
Nimble cosmeticians

Of inherited mediocrity, achieve
A short round of dismissive applause,
Or in witty conversation about nothing
Raise their game briefly to become
Really outstanding bores.

You may hardly credit it, but I,
I too, am of the company - yes,
Here at stark midnight, marring paper.
Incline your great head, Water Rat, since
We are brothers in this,

Though it is not Grey Rabbit nor any
Sensible purpose I toil for. Go home,
Give me peace, friend, that the world tonight
May acquire something to tut-tut at:
I must finish the poem.

No Metaphor

There is no metaphor:
The acorn's crammed with oak, the flower
Acts its one mask for ever; beasts
Tramp the blood's round.

Oh, the body withers, granted -
Gouty as thorn, crestfallen
As blown tulips; the eye runs and glazes
Like an old mastiff's:

But the spirit - call it that -
Compassed on some star wayfares
Out of the clock's duchy, drinks
Heart's drought, burgeons

Under a bone-dry wind.
Rage, time. To be shaken is nothing,
To be plucked. One speaks, shines, one is spent,
But not for your spoil.

Cancel me then. Dust's heel grind
My name's moment. In the desert love fed me,
Song and mercy. I glanced like a bird
Upon God's palaces.

Excavation in Borneo

Swifts through the great cave come and go
And cry interminably. The air is all
Bird-voices, wing-beat; and the floor below
Rank droppings, bone-meal. High upon each wall
Nests full of hairless young. We kneel and trace
A lost, vestigial race.

Time, the blind sexton, dug them deeply in
And we must mine for them. They fell like trees,
Leaving no carven word. But now we win
With spade and brush their meagre legacies -
Fragmented earthen pots, axe-heads entire,
The carbon of a fire.

And here, ah here, the warm dust falls away
From sheer unbroken colonnade, from white
Turret and arch and buttress. We survey
The relic of a man - bones stiff and light
As dried-out twigs, with nothing left to dress
This final nakedness.

We pause in silence. Now we could conceive
This frame our own, scavenged of flesh and mind,
Or Adam's, who in Eden before Eve
Cut syllables upon the virgin wind
To name the beasts. We pause and apprehend
The universal end,

Kneeling for him who on these girders hung
Pain and perplexity, who dwelt abstracted
On the fringed eyelids of his sleeping young
And lacked for words; who in his blood enacted
Rites of compassion, so that beast and flower
Shrank back into their hour,

Fearing his look, the pity of his hand.
But he fared on, encompassed with his tears,
Over an innocent and kingless land,
And heard the voices of the captured years
Ringing and falling. Us unborn he heard
And death, the organ-word.

August

Spring restates the case - a voice,
A rally of spears: you
Will believe then, move
Mountains. Winter even
Exhilarates, conceding
Blood its victory: and autumn
Has cogent passages, the dying fall.

But summer, starting well,
Slips into this vein of
Jaded rhetoric, a sort of
Senile iteration -
The gnawed and spiny leaves
Gesturing weakly
Over a fag-end of impulse.

And yet some see it otherwise:
Having rattled so many
Locked doors, they make
This place their peace. A woman
With cracked voice praises
The dusty miracle;
An old man kneels to touch the grass.

Curtain Calls

The instruments, having finished their chores,
Give Haydn a personal round of applause
In partial settlement of old scores.

Taking his curtain, Brahms
(A little tipsy) salaams,
Then starts an elephantine dance.

Beethoven, cross and dressed anyhow,
With a curt gesture summons in now
All his tattered manuscripts to take a bow.

Mozart - so little time! - thinks he will try
To escape, but is dragged onstage by
Hundreds of chords no more than knee-high.

Finally Bach - they played his No. 2 Suite
(No lyric, man, but get that beat!) -
Brings every brick in the building to its feet.

A Child Reads in Church

The age and weight and sorrow of the stone;
The window's unstanched wound; the unmuted
Organ savaging the air, a last clenched chord
Dashed in the face of silence for her cue.
To the old lectern she goes out alone.

Where was there such a stage, so lit, so mounted,
So propertied as this? Where such a script?
What player better cast than she, who from
Ten summers' tally senses like a storm
The taste of wrongs unsuffered and uncounted,

Who marks the guilt, the devils that assail,
And in her timid heritage salutes
The sweet untrammelled words? The flag furls out:
She at the lectern of a mortal day
In utter faith proclaims the household tale.

She reads from the ancient story; and the text
Describes her light and lucid voice upon
Hymn-shadowed quiet. The asseveration now -
'Lo, I am with you always' - mystery,
Reached from one generation to the next,

Flute-clear on her fresh lips and, as she ends,
Cathartic in the pause. We, we say nothing,
Resigned that at all times, at every turn,
Such chastisement may fall: and each without
The flicker of an eyelid apprehends

Once more how every day against a brother
The sword is raised. We walk into the sun:
The wrought leaf speaks, the populated grass
Murmurs its axioms. What should we say?
How shall we set one brick upon another?

Tenant

Set will to its employment. Mortify
The importuning flesh. Withdraw in turn
Sleep, food, distraction; let the senses burn
Ungratified in full celibacy.

Be memory suspended, love and fear,
The wits' resource and reason's juggling skill -
Yes, bid the champing intellect be still:
There is, we postulate, a spirit here.

I do not mean the self that passions wring,
That takes the lash and thinks itself divine,
That deals unendingly in mine and thine,
And scolds and plots; the self's a lesser thing.

The spirit that I speak of ruminates
All stuff the agent faculties ingest,
Metabolizes all and will not rest:
Its hunger never, or its watch, abates.

But it is neutral; you will not engage it
In this affair or that. It marks with patience
The self's crude appetites and aspirations,
And nothing seems to move it or assuage it.

Neutral indeed - it will not volunteer
A verdict on your act or indecision.
But surely its mere silence is derision
And mocks at your hypocrisy and fear?

Eschew all thinking then, subdue all passion.
Flush out this thing from cover; let the creature
(So call it, faute de mieux) show its feature
And render its account in honest fashion.

So then; and wait. The ambush is prepared.
See now what you shall see. But eyes and ears
Catch nothing after all; no shape appears.
The game's too subtle to be lured and snared.

Call intellect again and speculate.
Perhaps the thing's an ailment of our being,
An epidemic fault that rifts the seeing;
A blind neurosis breeding to negate.

Again - less sinister - it might be seen as
An antibody bred in and transmitted
To compensate the carnal and committed,
Bent on perpetuation of the genus.

Or God. It may be God. By which I mean
The unflawed plane that time's abraded on,
The adamant, the pole; that which alone
Stands at the centre, guarded and serene,
Subtending all the distance; the exact
Fine passion, the dispassionate core of love,
That neither tortures nor affections move:
The unsuborned and uncorrupted fact.

I cannot judge. I cannot. It preserves
Its namelessness, the spirit, but it gives
A name and signature to all that lives,
And never from its perfect progress swerves.

Its look through mortal eyes is never quelled
Although it lights on death. The spirit traces
The shape of crumbled things, forgotten faces,
Remembers how the tree stood, that was felled;

And us, the self of us, peripheral,
That cries to be perceived, it brings within
Some kind of pale, I think, some discipline.
I cannot judge. I cannot judge at all.

Gulls

The ploughed field is a rough square.
At its centre, the one on a dice,
The white gulls in a solid ring
Cluster, as if in conference there.

Like emissaries, some fly hence;
More float in singly to alight:
And all move within frontiers drawn
By danger and expedience.

That world's rim is a near cry.
They are simply the way they came,
Garmented by it, beak and feather -
Wind-riders of implacable eye.

They call harshly, squint from the cell
And heartland of what they are
At the sand-grain kingdoms whose
Circumferences touch theirs, repel:

Sand-grain realms, that breed and span
All that has been and becomes;
Circle upon circle, from the worm
And the ant in the furrow to man.

Circle upon circle. Each surmises
The rest contingent, peripheral.
Man chiefly, sure of lordship;
He names, lists, moralises.

Subtler he is than the gull
But less complete; for the bird's
Cogitation and instinct are one,
Helmeted as smooth to the skull

As its oilskin cap of feather,
History not ruminated but
Ingested to the point where
Act and purpose run together.

But man - is he at quarrel within?
Compassless with his desires,
Chasing so many norths, he seems
Uncertain what he should begin.

When were the poisons fed him?
Did some dark mistletoe thing
Set tap in his sense? For how
Could mere time have misbred him?

Faculty was offered him to speak
For the creation, embrace it
Whole in his hoop of knowing
And cherish all, strong and weak.

But he broke faith somehow. They say
Pride overtilted the balance
And the white myth slid from him,
Dream-like. Be that as it may,

Something on the journey occurred,
Some self-betrayal he now
Cannot forget or remember;
A choice was his and he erred.

He became the way he took,
Deformed by the error, his arts
Wilful to the manage, his love's
Flaw piteous in his look.

Piteous: but the powers still tread
And intone their theme in him
Obstinately. Fragments, as if
By chance, in his hand re-wed.
For it is integers at each last
That catch at him, all fulnesses -

Carved things and completed rhymes,
The year's tight loop holding fast

Near-perfections that require
Him perfect, to be perfect. Could he
Sip at his essence now, he might
Make everything again entire,

Feel the air run pure again
In his nostrils, the spirit
Fit like a cap to his will:
He would speak with all tongues then

Over all boundaries. For him
Time is no more than the road
To illusion and back. O birds,
Patient through this interim,

Whose knowledge is sheer being, worn
Truer than thought, closer than
Feather to feather, you shall at
The moment of his return,

Bodying forth the way you came,
Be that moment. I imagine
You rising to fly then, at once
Breaking in sunburst to proclaim

Wonder, as of a fifth season
Or a new annunciation
Whispered to being, into its grain,
Beyond reason and unreason -

Mere flesh with the joy made one,
End, beginning. And the sweet
Harshness of your cry goes echoing
Through all kingdoms, on and on.

Table

A thought of table was the start:
The prototype, and last the name,
Sequential in that order came,
A simple breathing-space apart.

The act of table then recurred
Uncounted times; and since, there's been
A mist of centuries between
The thing of table and the word.

And as with tables, so with chairs
And charity and grief and hate
And all pertaining to the great
Wide firmament of men's affairs -

The name's no more the accolade
It started as; the pristine thought,
That framed the vocables and caught
Each quiddity, is much decayed.

O at what Fall what fell? Or do
The long roads of attrition tire
The joy that trembles like desire,
The faith that labours to be true?

Bind hands and pray. The splintered stars
May yet run back into the first
Unblemished sphere from which they burst,
All sundered things throw off their scars

And journey home and be in place,
While tableness and chairhood win
What once was lost and new begin,
Love turn back to the first embrace.

As birds at gunshot break and fly
And scatter, and then shape anew
The ancient echelon, the true
Language of order in the sky,

So might it be, and time retrieve
The broken disciplines at length,
The unities, the sinless strength
Of Adam, and the look of Eve.

The Almond Tree

I planted that almond tree too near the house.
Spindly with shade it leans
To catch what meagre sun it may.
It blooms, but poorly, casts a few
Husked fruit into the grass:
But still it has outgrown you both, perhaps
Tiptoes for fuller sunlight, up and up.
Its leaves move gently, as it stands
Not without grace.

Children, there is a secret. It concerns
A thing that's now forgotten or is rather
Negatively remembered - for one knows
What it is not. What it is, is hidden
And will stay hidden.

But while I was talking
About the almond tree, my thought brushed something
Which shrank away. It owned
No category, texture, shape; it was
Perhaps a sport of memory, a thread
Torn from the past and clinging aimlessly
In a small angle of the mind. And yet
It could have been a rarer thing -
A mystery's shadow-form, correlative
To contemplation of the tree.

Children, this secret - but you do not listen;
Your eyes turn to the world, your hearts
Seek their own images of truth...

I set the tree there in my ignorance
And now there is no shifting it. The leaves
Redden and drop with some affliction:
A year or two, no more, and it will fail.
But while it lives, it seeks its nature.

How is this argued, would you say?
May one suppose
That this imperfect glorifies the perfect
In fruitless aspiration? Think also of
Plain women lacking love, the blackbird
Born wrong and dying for it, think of rocks
Baulked of their shape: all thwarted things
Chained to a flaw.
                                        Or - take it otherwise -
Are these the glorified, marked out to bear
Vicariously such suffering as their kind
Is subject to? But that would be nonsense -
Imperfect perfect, unfulfilled complete.

The tree grieves on insensibly.
The logic of it is despair; although,
As the sun strikes beyond the sickly leaves,
Logic is overridden. All that lives
Holds to its duty and participates,
Thriving or ailing, in the rite
Whose meaning is withheld; all, of its nature,
Keeps course, though lamed.
Thought circles always
Back to the rock-face scratched
With the old legend 'Love, and judge not.'

Children! But you have gone. And you must march
Against the banners of the world and tread
Upon the serpent, death.
Be of good heart.

Battle Orders

Nothing was written in the orders
But 'Fight'. We obey,
Clumsy but obstinate, contesting
This position, that; risking
Occasional foray:

Beaten back, desperate often,
Yet in a flash stirred
To new anger; changing sides even;
But shy of manifesto, handling
Warily each word.

And ever the man goes on
Behind his thought
Through the vagaries of fickle
Inward weather, love moving him,
Love's lack and doubt,

Love's whim and gift, but always
Dour and resisting:
Strong in weakness, he outfaces
The merely strong, and wins by
Simply existing.

Wins? But what is ever plainly
There to be won,
Except the clarity of the heart?
Wrestle for that. And finally, no
Bitterness, none.

Trouvaille

The search ended here. I had had no inkling,
Truthfully, that I sought; nor had I even known
There was this to look for, or indeed anything
Remotely comparable. Rather was it shown,

Vouchsafed, than that I found it - a convergence
Into one brief lucidity, engendered
Somehow in the algebra of circumstance,
Gathered up, held and momentarily tendered.

There was not, however, and one could not have
expected
Any tangible outcome: the thing was not for possession,
At least in the sense commonly accepted,
Or its simple meaning for rational expression.

You see, this was a mental event, no more,
And in one mind only, though not thereby
Essentially diminished; but even in metaphor
Its dimensions alone were hard to specify.

Even in metaphor: though I would say that chiefly
It smote me like spring's February patrol, when high
In city squares upon soiled ledges briefly
Birds squabble, and then suddenly their cry

Lifts like a faith. The needle had found north
And there was, incredibly, a fact, a destination.
The search had ended. The faculties might henceforth
Occupy themselves otherwise - in contemplation,

Talk, pastime, sorrow, tolerate the years' lapse
And all trivialities. Self's ultimate reason
Was in that hour met and saluted, as perhaps
Never again. The heart had outpaced its season

And seen incontrovertibles, miracle, joy's
Quick counter-glance, the charmed deer unpursued
Running silently, heard out of the air some voice
Whisper 'Yes, you are right; it is renewed.'

War - "Tank after tank in line"

November 4th. 1941

Wilfred Owen, the poet, died by the Sambre Canal
Seven days before peace; with his men trying to cross
The canal and the mad guns tearing the meadow
And all men aching for peace. Casually killed
By somebody's bullet he fell by the Sambre Canal
Twenty-three years ago.

The hand and the voice of Wilfred Owen were stilled.
It was dramatic enough, the soft lead sent
Into the yielding body, the brave
Innocent assassin tearing out of the precious book
A pageant of singing words; defeat of glory
That a moved finger gave.

But I am not mourning him now; nor will I dare
Call it untimely how he was struck, how his eyes
Were shut to the sunlight, this lover
Of men, this poet. Others, a million, died also.
They are part of the soil the foot strikes; part of the soil
Which the swift grasses cover,

O part of the soil which I say is no soil but the quick
Warm quivering fibre of bodies. For it was not time
For these ignorant children to die,
For these half-grown men to be cold. The dust stirs and rebels
Remembering the blood's flowing and warmth, the hand's power,
The strong hinges of the thigh.

No: only the trivial is said and is left to say.
Wilfred Owen died so. This evening I read his poems.
He would have written more. Let me mourn
Not the fingers gone nerveless, the heart broken and stopped,
Only the words unwedded, the alphabet sprawling,
The poems that could not be born.

Dog Two Able

We swung on round the S-bend in the track,
Tank after tank in line, heading for home.
Trailing a dust-cloud that the sun spun gold;
Monsters by cornfield, landscape of our time.

And I looked down at Dog Two Able's guns -
The black MGs, the silver seventyfive:
I dreamed of peace as no good soldier should,
Of true men dead and hypocrites alive.

O Dog Two Able, in your armour rides
All that the past hoped and the future holds,
All gentleness and justice - keep them safe,
Speed on the stroke that scavenges and builds!

O Love, though now your song be cannonade,
Yet shall the theme be altered - yet shall peace
Thunder her motive in, a music lift
Which through the generations shall not cease.

Spectator

"Tally ho!" the plump captain
Shouted. "Kill the bastards!"
To me at least, it seemed
Gratingly outre, something that belonged
To a species of poor literature.

Being in the troop, however,
I really had no choice
But to go along. What would the enemy
Think if they could understand it? I
Muttered a prim disclaimer.

Life was like that. It appeared
Credible enough at a distance
Or in reported speech, but on direct
Experience melodramatic when not
Mannered and humdrum.

How to describe it? As if
Wandering backstage one stumbled
Suddenly from the wings
Into a play's action and had to
Ad lib desperately.

The others have their script.
I must admire their
Technique and fluency,
How they fill out their skins and clothes and move
The dialectic on.

Oh, I assume a role
To escape notice. I smiled,
Travelled, formed views on
Time, rice-pudding, the existence of God.
But I didn't do it well.

The captain got a medal -
His kind of Oscar. Others
Had their minor awards -
Money, ulcers, pregnancy, obituaries,
Citations for long service.

But I heard no clapping.
There was possibly no audience;
And in any case the scenes
Never ended tidily. The thing had no
Aesthetic coherence.

Let me withdraw from the stage,
Backing away like the butler
Who brought an envelope,
Contents trivial, on a shiny salver.
I shall not be missed.

In Memoriam

A little earth disturbed, a white wood cross
Tell that a sapper died among these trees.
Fresh and brown grave cut in the vivid grass:
We passing on a road to the Volturno.

Do such men dying hand on to their comrades
The wealth of their desire for home? It seems
So bright a thing to fail: but this too fades,
I suppose, is cancelled with the body.

And yet when we swing landwards to Liverpool,
Southampton, Greenock or past the Dover cliff,
In us like a guilt it will be, a cruel
Hand on our joy's shoulder, such men's longing;

And there will be in the memory for always
A white wood cross, near the road where a poor
Ragged and hungry crew of children plays.
'Death in the midst of life', it might be said.

Conversation 1964 - "The power requires its emblem"

Conversation 1964

Close that south window from the rain which sings
On the parched palate of our clay. The seedlings
Tremble, drink. My four young poplars lean
Delicately to the east. Ants from their foraging
Turn back for home. And under the rustling hedge
Birds rummage or just stand - the common sort,
All fathered in this acre - blackbird, wren,
Sparrow and thrush; such scuffle of small wings

And darting talk. One tap upon the pane
And they'd be off - frail, eager, nervous life
Bent on and on, serving some secret will
We may not penetrate, some essay in
Another style. They launch my thoughts to seek
A June three years behind when, wandering
On the green rampart of Old Winchester Hill,
Where the chalk muttered with late-fallen rain,

I saw a lark in fathoms of deep air
Climb, climb to utter - and I hear it now,
Over the smooth tumulus that desperate song -
The stored cry of the years (for so to me
In that calm place it seemed), the ripened pain
And aspiration of the anxious dust.
You smile at that; and Teilhard could be wrong,
Who shone a candle upon Darwin's stair,

Thinking the very atoms bore God's brand
And swung to holy north; who posited
That, folded in itself, the basic stuff
Cohered and bloomed. His argument ran on,
Faith leading rhetoric - as you would say,
The blind the blind - all the way home. And yet
To gasp and shake the head is not enough:
Though truth's to suffer, not to understand,

Yet each excogitates his heaven and plays
Mere life as the first act - thus Jung, who spoke
Of the dour rootstock nourished in the dark,
How it gropes upward in its chosen spring,
Greeting the day as if the shoot were some
Apocalyptic mouth: and this he held
Emblem of mind, as I conceive my lark
Told the earth's thought in humble paraphrase.

We come back to our birds. Remember how
Eiseley, seeking stock, chanced on those hawks
In the deserted hut. The female fled.
The male he seized and caged: when morning came,
He took it in his hand and met its eye
And read the creature's spirit, hopeless yet
High and invulnerable, undiscomfited,
But taut against him like a tested vow.

What else could pass from look to look? These were
Strangers without a language and committed
Beyond all will or wish to separate ways.
He felt its heart pound on; then, with a sigh,
Set it down gently in the meagre grass.
It lay unstirring on its breast, perhaps
Dreaming captivity still beneath the day's
Temperate glance and studying despair.

Then, swifter than the eye could grasp, it was gone,
Arrowing up; and higher, as from the sun,
A knife-thrust cry, as she who hour on hour
Had hung in patience plunged. Still the male soared
Headlong, her passion's challenger, through great
Parabolas of joy. In duel of love
Fiercely they tilted then, and where no more
The searching eye could hold them wheeled and spun,

Darted and hovered in their dance, and tossed
Question and answer down the empty sky.
Love was the home she summoned to, the fire
Kindled at need, the flag to rally on,
The way that led con brio to the end.
That way they took, uncompassed. Eiseley's heart
Reeled still with her first cry, as on his ear
Their voices rose and dwindled and were lost.

But this was long ago. Among the high
Glacial pastures, where the sandstone ranges
In cliffs and rifts, the eggshell bones are ground
By predatory gales; on naked plains
The feathers rot in piles of tumbleweed:
Here the snows visit and the sun devours
The juices of all flesh. Time's sleep has drowned
All but one memory of that passionate cry.

Time's sleep: the taciturn and rawboned hills,
Great shoulders hunched, snore on. He, Eiseley,
Reining his horse upon that table-land,
Dismounted, knelt, and on the earth's wide breast
Sought as for treasure; took into his hands
Stalks and rock-bones, crystalline pebbles chafed
Smooth in an old sea-world, bright crumbs of sand:
And each, as if some tireless, lonely skill

Had hewn it singly, dwelt within such form
As was its only speech. But there was more,
Something that crowned all this. What cried? What sang?
Who broke the perfect primal integer,
So that the halves, both rendered name and need
And greater than the whole, remarry thus
In spasm of joy, as lightning in its pang
Arcs cloud to cloud through vacancies of storm?

He rode away and took the passes down;
And there's the tale. You smile again, I see.
Yes, I select such theses as sustain
My prejudice and hope: and who does not?
Philosophy's engendered in the heart,
Not in the mind, and hunts shop-windows for
The arguments it needs. But look, the rain
Breaks suddenly, and there's a rainbow thrown

Above the shining roofs; fire, water, air -
Gayer geometry than Carter taught.
I toy with private fancies: all those gods
That populate the index, who in myth
Rubbed shoulders with poor mortals and begot
Heroes from girls, their splendid goddesses
With cloud-grey eyes - could they, against the odds,
Have trodden the young earth? Perhaps they were

Delegates of the ultimate power, sent
Like man writ large to guide the simple thoughts
Of simple folk towards infinity:
Pugnacious, jealous, lustful, covetous,
And whimsical as chance, yet with panache
And a quick eye for the magnanimous, they
Taught the first lessons - awe, humility
And resignation to their chastisement.

These delegates withdrew - Marduk and Jove,
Ahura and the rest - either in some
Ordered demarche or as wild creatures run
When the air menaces; and we were left
To face the storm of Christ. Yes, we endured,
Although the lightning dazzled us and lit
Landscapes unguessed: we drudge and fumble on,
Sad-countenanced apprentices to love.

Hand goes to hand, but there's a word unsaid:
See how the fingers gnarl beneath my touch,
How the hair whitens. What do I destroy -
Not filled, not quenched, though I consume the world?
And nothing's left to hold against the breast,
No eye keeps faith or seeks the truth of us.
Somehow to fare on, past the final buoy
Drifting without an oar, unprovendered,

Somehow to lash the spirit to the frame
And make on through the cold: no less is asked.
No counter-pledge; save that our home, our grace -
Zu ahnen nur, nicht kennen - these may yet
Breathe like a presence when some chemistry
Of place and mood employs us, when we turn
On crag or crowded street as if to face
Something that would have called us by a name

No christening bestowed. You have felt this? -
The sense that past our grasping it is well,
That rock and artefact and creature stand
Each fitly on its plinth of being and all
The bricks of time lie squarely in their place.
Strange and not strange: a brightness flickers on
Some yet unshrivelled foliage in the mind;
Words stir at the tongue's root. Call it neurosis,

Delusion, affectation, what you choose:
I mount no argument, no longer ask
The reason for these things. Have you felt too
This need for loneliness, to cast the halter,
Not of the half-truths only and the offence
We hourly do our fellows, but of all
The weary iteration we toil through,
The games of intellect we always lose,

The self abrading self? How one could brood
In those green hinterlands, where boulders poise
Crouched in the glacier's wake and rivers run
In sinewy unconcern; or lizard-like
Move with the naked rudimentary powers,
Marching and halting with the sap-flow, turned
To statuary in the cold, and in the sun
Responsive to the shifting of the blood.

Jung grasped this paradox - the weaned desire,
The acorn growth into identity
Prerequisite of love; and the blurred face
That looks up like a mermaid from the flux
To lure the gazer down. These powers contend
Each to possess the man; and he must yield,
Though never utterly, to each embrace,
Would he achieve himself. But whence this fire

That leaps unkindled out of common air?
Behind us those long echelons of the dead
Lie with their solved equation. They would tell
That youth and age are nothing, how the gift
Choose with dice but will not be denied,
At prayer or bidding neither comes nor stays:
Blake with his angels; Wordsworth like a bell
Rung over Cumberland; bewildered Clare,

Whom madness could not silence; Coleridge,
'Dear Coleridge', alone on that wide sea,
Who met death's sad reflecting eye, his great
Synopsis still unshaped and, with bowed head
Granting his sloth, won like the prodigal
A wordless clasp; Yeats, driving like a prow
Through ebbing days, who steered his battened freight
Into the darkness, scorning anchorage.

The power requires its emblem - tiger, deer,
Or, as the Roman carved undyingness,
A cone grasped by a snake: and yet a bird,
Swung from the bough's trapeze, evokes it well -
Eiseley's sparrowhawks, the struggling lark,
A wingspread eagle mapping continents,
Or those small flutterers of ours bestirred
About the feathery tarmarisk, that fear

The tappings on the pane. Their bones are built
Of earthborn stuff and sippings from the stream
But cored with air to float their element.
Even the aborted thrush that hatched in spring -
Lame, broken-winged - sustains the metaphor:
It tried to hop, to peck, to hoist itself,
And failing was yet thrush, and thrush it went
Though songless down. Blood, beak and feathers spilt

Past pity's help, the wretched ounce fell blind
Into the grave we scratched, to rot for some
Far resurrection's sake. Its fellows fly,
Fly on and turn upon the wing and keep
No tally of the dead; they drink the rain,
Wear the light's plumage, glancing down as if
To mediate between the earth and sky,
And cast their glittering songs upon the wind.

Voices among the poplars - thrushes, men -
Rising and dying: what they truly utter,
Above mere business of mortality,
Why, none will know. And Jung is gone, and Teilhard
Reads the last wisdom now, of bread or dust.
What moved us, love or fear? Were we defeated?
Open the window, let the smell of tree
And earth come in. Now, let us try again.

London Scenes - "Each passer wise with the world"

London: Autumn

On the slow Thames my thought
Drives like a barge or hangs
In a cluster of swans:
I stand on every roof
Watching the sunset's
Smoke and bronze.

Migratory birds wheel,
Dark gestures above
Steeple and tower:
I as for penance hold
The spent workday's rout,
This tumbling hour.

Shrink, shrink, my season.
The leaves drift: a beggar
Wraps round his ears
A shabby coat and plays,
Invoking for a coin
The shrivelled years.

And you, sad-face, o city,
Grey where the shadows
Grope now and climb,
Soiled, badged with lights,
Beautiful under the
Hammer of time -

Counting the tides, you also
Sense your term as the wind
Runs high and cold.
Bridge-leap, flowers in stone,
Tenement, carved king;
The pass is sold.

Hungerford Bridge

Three years. I cross the river once again.
I greet you, London, and I feel your pain.

Old crippled beast, you squat beneath the sky,
And cannot run or hibernate or die.

Trains shake the bridge: Thames sifts the mud below.
An anchored boat rocks gently to and fro.

Lit windows in the darkened walls burn on,
Like script in cuneiform upon a stone.

The message is not hope. Each concrete page
Proclaims the grief of a defeated age -

Or so it seems, defeat. Perhaps we all
Fell equally from grace, and deeper fall.

Time did not, as we thought it would, unfold;
The ingenious stars were not to be cajoled.

I pause, recalling how I loved this city:
The wind drops down and night comes on like pity.

The famous towers bathe still in yellow light;
But one beam strays to rake the frosty night.

High aerials listen and the radars turn.
What sign, what presences, do they discern?

Is the old guardian benediction broken?
The harsh voice of the god, has it finally spoken?

I turn to go. This sad familiar place
Holds the imperfect beauty of a face -

Yet thus imperfect, perfect: every weather
Binds us afresh, and we endure together.

Moon shadow falls upon the bridge's lee,
As moss grows on the north side of a tree:

Tomorrow sun, or monotone of rain.
Three years like broken promises. Again
I greet you, London, and I feel your pain.

Lincoln's Inn Fields

Great Turnstile pours the chattering hundreds in,
Strollers at summer noon,
Who pause to smile at Vicky's new cartoon
Here at the Statesman or,
A step or two before,
Peer through the glass at her who sits within -

The tender vision throned in Ganymed,
Grave with young tilted nose;
Where Breughel, Klee and Gauguin hang in rows
For loiterers to appraise,
And shadowy Rembrandt says
Self-pictured, 'Heed me, friend, though I am dead.'

But now on Newman's Row one turns the back,
Hearing the orator fling
Cliché on cliché to a flippant ring,
Or veering right to where
In Soane's sepulchral air
The Hogarths pose among the bric-à-brac.

Look, thousands wander where the plane trees wade
In lakes of lilting grass;
Smoothly the burgeoning girls like schooners pass,
Dressed overall, or here
At anchor lie and bear
The cargo of their sex in sun and shade.

This gentle idle commerce turns the day
Upon its hinge. The throng
Thins at each clock-voice, and along
Green-skirted walks the true
Processors take their cue
To infiltrate the cool and dappled way.

So this old mumbling woman now in torn
And mangy fur reclines
A bench's length. A bearded patriarch dines
Out of a newspaper or reads
Verses that no-one heeds.
Frail creatures that the times have warped and worn.

And one I mark who takes his usual seat
With timid vacant glance;
Cloth cap, white head, of no significance
Save to the flock that comes
Daily to peck the crumbs
He brings with him and scatters at his feet.

Pigeon and sparrow celebrate his whim.
If love's no more than need
Known and reciprocated, here indeed
Admit it runs between
Those whom these alms convene -
Confident, shrewd, insatiable - and him,

Who long ago put by the tedious book
Of the time's pride and rage
And wandered out into the curtilage
Of his self-banishment to praise
The swift's trajectory or raise
To the huge arrowing swan his hungry look.

His eyes deny me more. I shall not know
If he acts god upon
A microcosm of innocence undone,
Leaning as from the sky
To shake his head and sigh
Grief at the feathered trespasses below;

Or if in ultimate deference he crumbles
Bread of a sacrament -
Token of penance for the knees unbent,
The flask of tears unwept,
The homage that had slept

Withheld from one towards whom his thought now stumbles.

Dear angel of this place, who grant it still
Feature and breath and stand
Guard at the seven entrances; whose hand
Shakes not in storm, whose faith
Prints laughter upon death;
Small delegate of the conceiving will:

Comfort him yet. Sustain us all who go
Beneath your arm and pass
The sweet carved children. From the day's distress,
The barricaded grief,
Render each heart relief
In your cool anteroom of shape and hue.

Yet so dispose the boughs that move outside
Symmetry into grace,
The grass's equipoise of growth and peace;
So pleasure us, so bless
Man in his loneliness
And with your mild correction touch his pride.

Graffiti

'Cock was here.' 'I like a boy in tight jeans.'
'Touch me up, Sandra.' And a gallery of the parts -
Great crevices of tumbled girls, the tall
Phalli in their ritual stance like menhirs -
Done as from life, pudenda in flagrante,
By the anonymous masters of such arts.

Overstated, of course. But this genre
Moves with assurance in a crisp idiom between
Dream and reality. The draughtsmanship
Has swift and lapidary force; the text,
Florid or exclamatory, is always
Eventful and undilutedly obscene.

But do not miss the irony. Each artist
Has pierced the superficies to set down
His vision and his judgment. He has stripped
The population of all garb, all mores,
Construed it simply as a herd of creatures
Carting their genitalia round the town.

Has anyone written a history of this business?
The stricken bird-man painted at Lascaux,
The dancing wizards of Trois Freres, all flourish
Shrewd weapons at en garde in blatant
Exhibitionism. These date from
Some ten or fifteen thousand years ago.

The later evidence is much eroded.
But faith was kept; it must have been. Through all
The tyrannies that trampled poets down
This licence, this impertinence, evaded
The rod and fiat. There were always these
Profanities upon some stinking wall.

One must, I think, concede it: common bawdy
And lechery channel the same sap that fires
The outgrope of the spirit; this great spectrum
Is not to be blanked off at either end.
The mean is mean; and the full man must speak
From his whole count of torments and desires.

So the farting dwarf fights on, back to back
With the embattled angel: against the odds
They have stood up before the host of dismay.
Limbs hacked, eyes blinded, they have neither yielded
Nor lamented, but suffer loss together.
Their deed shall be acceptable to the gods.

What did the cold fingers write? A face is drawn
Of calm and anger; the legend 'Cast out fear.'
'Love', 'love' recurs, carved on the sword-hilt, scratched
On the rock; the names of men, songs, seasons -
Ancestral words. And there, among them scribbled,
Look, the old affirmation, 'Dick was here.'

Girl in a London Square

Rather a small story for a god:
But ripening, past fifteen, she balances
Shyly on towering heels,
(Warm currents, trade winds - where's the metaphor?)
As from the rocking belfries of the sun
The hour, the new-born, peals.

See, lesser actors move and take her eye:
A beetle tramps the path, the spider scales
High battlements of air;
A bird ferries its slight beating heart
Above the city's voice; and walkers-on
Thread the green square.

Rise, girl, it is your cue; the minute runs.
Settle your dress, your face, the curl that sits
Bravely behind your ear.
This is your entrance: will them all to turn
And fall to silence. Launch the carrying words,
Now - 'I am here, I am here!'

Diary

June 10th. I could try it for a while, the
Unelaborated recording of trivia -
Episodes, casual fancies; confine it
To a few dozen words a day. A flypaper,
As it were, hanging out to catch what comes
Or a kind of therapy.

June 11th. One must do this without contrivance,
Without (how difficult!) striking attitudes. There was haze
Over the river this morning, and London
Looked positively oriental. We moved up
Like the Chinese army in disguise. There
Was no resistance.

June 12th. I walked back over the bridge.
London, I have worn out your pavements, I
Am answerable for you somehow. You are
Tranquil and sordid and complaisant.
The old beggar was there (is he real?) The buildings
Gazed at the sunset.

June 13th. The irises are fading; the red may's
Rusty but still brave. A card from Jurgen -
In Salzburg, but remembering Surrey.
Give thanks for our island, its cool palm
Upon each brow. Where we are dead, shall we weep,
Forgetting this greenness?

June 14th. Two lovers were kissing at the bus-stop.
What wisdom is there to offer such as these?
Hearts brim unaccountably. O let them brim!
And the plane trees - after a winter reticence,
Passages of such beauty, the leaves'
Intricacy, the stance.

June 20th. I must not let this lapse again;
The trap has to be kept baited. I sat
Under the plane trees. 'To live in time',
'To be oneself', 'to love' - what statement is not
A kind of tautology? There was thunder,
A pointillist rain.

June 21st. Love is the purpose and the trophy; but
All love is appetite, even the love of God.
Ergo, there is no good. Yet I cannot
Live with that thesis; therefore it is wrong.
Why does our logic pink us like a smugly
Expert duellist?

June 22nd. Leaves shifting in the sun. Under compulsion
The bird turns in the sky and the river winds;
No act, no word autonomous. Even mockery
Is mere connivance. There is something in the air
I cannot breathe. Something unidentified
Goes by default.

June 26th. I stood on the bridge. In autumn
Birds will gather in multitudes over the river
As they have always done, and we shall watch them.
I thought of the city with compassion. I thought
Of Pasternak's 'convoy of barges' - the centuries
Coming to be judged.

June 27th. This is where Shakespeare walked. He wrote
Of reconciliation and, I suppose, hope
In the last plays, but was silent afterwards.
How was it at the end? If you are not
Weatherboarded with impenetrable dogma,
Does the storm come in?

June 28th. But nothing will happen until we judge;
That judgment is the event. There was rain,
Rain like repentance, and I saw the barges
Nose through it, shining; as if the imperative
Were obstinately to move and reject and
Still hold course, hold course.

July 1st. But are not all theses parochial,
Local in time as vegetation, conditioned by
Topography and sun? Can the compass ever
Swing, as it seems to, to a mind's eye north,
A Gebiet of non-history that nourishes
Unshrivelling truth?

Truth - not a subject and predicate thing, nor even
A mental affirmation; a forswearing rather,
An abstention from the syllabus, a bald
Non sequitur, an anonymous
Illegible but decisive reservation
Scored in the margin.

July 4th. It is no use. How many cities were there
That seemed eternal? How many middle-aged men,
And better poets, apostrophised them? I see
On Thames' loop this dear Babylon, the tentative faces,
Their purpose as that of the swimmer before
He yields to the wave.

July 5th. Last entry. What is there for publication?
The judgments are intuitive, always provisional,
Probably wrong; the love predatory, combative;
Everything partial or flawed. There is only
The unblurred poignancy of time passing,
Deleting, scavenging;

And the sense of something quite incredibly held
Against the tides; as if a voice countered,
Dispassionately, the dogmas of transience:
Though for the rustle of leaves, the incessant
Riverdrops' jostle and crumbling grind of old mortars
I cannot hear it.

Beggar on Hungerford Bridge

Clockface, hurrying feet,
Each passer wise with the world;
See how their ships disdain
The water, how they have hurled
Steeples overhead, contrived
This sculpted youth: while I
Balance - no more - between
Earth racing, turning sky.

So, we avert our look.
How should those waning eyes
Chafe us with judgment?
Sipping our doom, he dies,
Chained to our grief; but still
Hears as God may hear
The soul's silence, the pulse's
Metronome of fear.

A coin shines in a puddle;
The river bears away
Spent images, rain, tears,
Driftwood, the time of day:
And lovers by the lamps,
Credulous, entwined
In madness there among
The flagellant hearts, walk blind.

Love - "All my hope and home and end"

Pictures

Pictures of hanging men and women tortured;
Prisoners, prisoners; the shattered hull of towns;
Bombs diving that the camera saw and shows
But could not halt - blood through the veins

Returning to the earth's heart, having fed
Mad limbs. And there you smooth your dress:
And I recall the beauty of your shoulders,
Your friendship, your warm skin's softness...

Pictures all ghosted upon your picture -
Bombs dropping through dark tears, shadows
Of broken bodies on your shoulders, prisoners
Shuffling over the skirt a light wind blows.

The huge wheel grinds. But you have such a look
As crowds out memories which should be too great
To be so exiled...This is my tongue tampering
Where even heart cannot articulate.

Sonnet

I can remember the eyelid's motion,
The lips pursing, the puzzle in the eyes;
The neck arched and leaning, the contraction
Of the forehead. But I can visualise
All only as in a dream. I can see
Only the change and movement of the face,
Never the colours; there is no memory
Of the iris blue or green, never a trace.

And the flesh lingers finely on the bone
So short a while. And time will not endure
Such warm especial lustre in your look
Longer than countable days: but he will break
The union of that colour and this line,
Dam up this river's flow and quench that fire.

Love Song

The sun shows half-past seven on the clock,
Then sinks behind the chimney, his day done
As far as this hemisphere is concerned.
I think you are better than the sun.

Now there is one star over the police station
And two through the window over the vase;
One, two, three, four over the taxi-rank.
I think you are better than the stars.

Soon the sun and the stars will stop;
I too shall be accounted for:
Above all, you will finish. So there will be
Nothing very interesting any more.

Apprenticeship

Timid of quarrels, conscious of the stars,
The boy lived on; and memory retrieves
Football, the verse a casual book unbars
And Horsham church framed in the green of leaves.
While out beyond the skyline of his dream,
Dark-haired and neat, two hundred miles away,
So far from Roffey and the cricket team -
Would she set eyes on him? No one could say.

Somehow he came to her; and somehow then
She tried him as the finger strikes a key.
And who but she may tell what note she heard?
But he has won what is not lost again,
For love grew strong and gently as a tree,
Sun and rain in the leaves and a singing bird.

Guerrillas

Watching you laugh, I cannot think that age
Must some day on that victor grace prevail,
So brave the battle that your clear words wage
And with such fearlessness your eyes assail.

Yet Time shall conquer you and chain your foot,
Daub your brown hair with ashes of his grey,
Disarm the heart and capture for his loot
The flag of beauty that you bear today.

But though the forefront of your charge be lost,
Inspired guerrillas fighting in your name -
Such as one former look or the mere ghost
Of that old smile - shall strike with such a sting
That Time the tyrant will sit wondering
And know his sin and sink his head for shame.

Love (I)

The odd glitterings of becks
Are joined into the river's
Shining resolve. And I believe
That it is so with lovers;
That the separate wayward
Happinesses of hearts
Join to a dearer thing:
That we, whose love thus hurts,
Shall move as clear and deep -
Each life one with the other's -
As a strong river flows
Under the forest of stars.

Photograph

You see the young limbs in this photograph,
The small bare perfect foot; that strand of hair
Blown out as it may not be blown again;
The face so young bright in the photograph?

Soon, soon the face bright in this photograph,
So young beneath the gentleness of hair,
Will smile and mock these years of loneliness -
O who shall guess her from a photograph?

Separation

She turns. A hairstrand falls across her face.
And within and along and through there is all the blood's
Throbbing and sunlike blazing...
                                        She is all
My light and my warmth. She is all
My hope and home and end. And I am nowhere,
Playing with old pictures. I had as well
Talk to the ant and cricket or in fever
Lust after a phantom...
                              I am beating
My face against the bolted door of miles.

Tradition

So the head turns, the eye's quick rapier flickers,
The neck's architecture is joy abundant,
The grace caught is ancestral but new beyond belief:
And there blooms on the skin and burns beneath the eyelid
The immemorial blood of the fathers, holding the remarkable
Continuity of sharp excited grief.

So ever; for it is unchangeable that men
Always shall be astonished, abashed, bewildered,
Cast down at the inborn pride, the inherited gaze.
The years have wearied the steps of lovely unnumbered women,
Have erased the countless gestures; but to this the years
Cannot breed an indifference. Beauty will still amaze.

And now, simply because you are one of the beautiful,
So that men turn, and you know they turn, as they see you pass,
I want you to move to the sunlight a moment and stand;
That I may point and say, while the clock is poising his hammer,
'This is she that perplexed me with happiness and dejection,
The slender one with the selfish eyes and restless hand.'

Love (II)

Chance, darkening and shining like the light on leaves,
Moth-drab - then suddenly
Bright and hued as a butterfly;
Flung like a bottle where the wave heaves and lifts.

O eyes and heart that wandered for love like bees,
Tiptoe, for you have stumbled
Where cool she sleeps and naked;
The sun has changed like music on the waters.

When she awakes, her eyes shall show no shadow;
Her body's easy leisure
She will not hide; nor fear.
How is your plotting lust escaped or altered?

Strange, do you think, how your desire now kindles
To pride, eyes' wisdom?
Your philosophy becomes
Clear in her kiss, the movement of her breasts?

Marriage (I)

He swam in her blue gaze. Suddenly his pride
Broke like a rotten plank and he cried,
'Take me, heart's squalor, deceit and all,
Loose tongue and hobbled wing, or I fall
Into the whirlpool and spiral down
My self's black nothing to drown.'

She nodded then, contemptuous of despair.
He freighted her with all his waking care,
The merchandise of memory and pain.
She took it, took it as a blessing; and when
In dream he tossed and spoke aloud she smiled,
Clasping him like a child.

Body gave body peace. Drowsing she lay
Limp in this stranger's arms. She tried to pray
For coupling beasts, the foxes in the wood,
All creatures that by edict loved and stood
In the great trap. She failed and tried again,
But slept before Amen.

Marriage (II)

“Let others toss and shipwreck.You and I
Shall break the body’s bounds,” he said, “and grow
Hermaphrodite, one spirit and one breath –
Love’s prototype, unhaltered, undefiled!”
She did not wholly comprehend, but smiled.
“Here is my troth,” she answered, “until death.”

How could he have foreseen the rest? This throw
Fell short of paradise. But by and by
He learned how in simplicity she was wise,
That each was each and other, how no track
Climbed that last scree. He came to understand
The paradox, that what love first denies
In time is strangely rendered. Hand to hand
Great gentleness is given and given back.

To my Children

Under varnish of affected indolence
And a defensive scepticism I sensed
Love's quality, boy - an unformulated,
Untrumpeted vow to be ready
To stand in a narrow place and defend it
And be true for ever. I dreamt I lay
Helpless under gunshot and you
Rode up on a white horse to save me.
Whatever happens or does not, I say
That is your self, though you fail it,
Though the call go unheard or unuttered.

Girl, you I see unruffled in the fracas,
Reading the maps or with your endemic
Archaeological patience piecing together
Jigsaw fragments of sanity; like others
Appalled in the stuffy labyrinth, atremble
At the beast's roar, but your intelligence
Bobbing up on its keel of obstinacy
As you grope for the thread. Time silts us
But not your wit - may that ever apply
Its summary limiting statute to all
Humbug and rhetoric: promise me this.

Exhort is easier than perform; and the young
Smile behind their hand at exhortation.
I could say 'Let the spirit stand up and
Unequivocally announce itself, sequitur
And non sequitur embrace, the tears
Stream when they will, heart with a bon mot excuse
Time's gaucheries. Be in and of that lighted
Circle the nameless things go snarling round
And dare not enter.' But I will be silent,
Nor ever claim you now, except as each
Mortal claims any other. Do not deny me.

My Son

Boy in your sleep turning,
It is the fettered sea in your stopped ear
That sighs and pulses. Now it's gone
As the wind changes. Idly here
I muse as time strides on.

Hushed hands, blood unresting,
Is it grace or chaos you read
On the dark eyelid? Now
Your lips move dumbly to exclaim or plead,
The miracle of your brow

Interrogative, questing,
Even in sleep - unwasted
By loneliness or disbelief,
Though you have sipped misgiving and tasted
The autonomy of grief.

What is there worth the learning
To guide you to? What words confine
Not truth, mere wisdom in their cage?
The world that dents your pillow is not mine.
I pause before the page

As time's great presses turning
Print ceaselessly the sorrow
My hands cannot forfend.
The famous riddles wait for you. Tomorrow
Your masted heart shall bend

Stormwards to the testing.
May you through peril gain
The surf-blanched islands, never shifting course
As I have shifted, but past pain
Steering, beyond remorse,

To landfall on, investing
A stammering wildness
With the clear catalytic word.
Utter the obstinacy of the spirit's witness,
That it be for a moment heard

Above the mock and spurning,
The great cacophony
Of trifles that would smother
All that we are. Consider, there may be
In twenty years another

Child of this blood attesting
That faith beats on behind
The shame-faced treacheries
Of will and flesh. Him too I have in mind
Where under siege he lies,

Far in his sleep turning,
Walled by your arm, the old
Tempters encamped outside.
Loved, warm, tonight; alone through time and cold
Tomorrow he must ride.

Conversation 1975 - "That ground beyond time"

Conversation 1975

That what we loved should stale;
That that which cropped for us should be ploughed in;
That our old central faith which bloomed the more
For doubt and deviation should be lost;
That thought should yield its juridical pride,
Words cease their decent mediation, courage
Stumble and fail:

It is not possible. But here,
Watching beyond the Sandstrasse a wild
Mélange of traffic rolling endlessly,
Brutally agile, swift without intent,
I see it all - ungoverned, immoderate -
For symbol of the will: aggressive force
Mounted on fear.

Where, where then are we driven?
The growth was towards identity and name -
With purpose or without, but labouring on
From the first cell's division to assume
Form, gainliness, self-divination, thought,
And blossom for the fruit of personal love
Offered and given.

And man is the event
In which the years concentre and converse -
His mind the deed, reverberating back
Beyond blood's genealogies as far
As breeding earth. He speaks and, as it hears,
Creation sings in counterpoint or mourns
In dull dissent.

For plant and beast and stone,
With untaught grace, in every variant mode,
Raise their unwearied symbols to assert
Quintessences - a native shape, a mild
Propriety of being, faculties
Subtle with apprehension for
The air and sun:

They thrive or are oppressed
Beneath his tutelage, in whose full heart
The dark and light cohabit, in whose blood
The recollection swims of Adam's fall -
The man, each man alone, upright within
The landscape of his spirit, the entire
Myth in one breast.

His answer must be heard.
The summers do not sense their passing, blossom
Falls without grief, the beast confronts its end
In mere perplexity. But man knows death,
And fear divides him from himself unless
He grasps the ancient discipline and finds
The synoptic word.

Truth is that discipline;
The word is love, the ineluctable,
That answers to itself and stands its ground.
I think of Jägerstätter, quite alone,
But safe through fire in his simplicity;
Bonhoeffer, citadelled on gentleness,
Rock-sure within.

I think of the White Rose -
Students in Munich thirty years ago.
At Stadelheim one February day
I wandered searching path by path, as snow
(How bitterly it drove into the face)
Laid wreaths at every stone, and cypresses
Trembled and froze.

I could not find the grave;
And yet their lying there redeemed that place -
The earth, the squatting prison where they died,
All Germany. I knew the miracle,
And gave my thanks for it, of naked faith
Levelled at chaos, struck, but holding on
Through death to save.

For each one in his cell
Was obdurate. Hans wrote upon the wall -
'Allen Gewalten zum trotz sich erhalten'
Sophie had dreamed - 'Ich trug an einem sonnigen
Tag ein Kind' She handed the child safe,
Over a chasm opening at her feet;
Then only, fell.

These entered the high theme,
Matching Bonhoeffer's holy fortitude,
Franz Jägerstätter's inarticulate
Hunger for right beneath the eye of God -
Hans Scholl defiant, Sophie's joyful 'Das
Wird Wellen schlagen!' and her trust, that child
Nursed in a dream.

So to outflank defeat;
So to dismiss fear as irrelevance,
Aggression as despair; to see the self
Not, Mara, borne like flotsam on the wave
Of some chill social tide, but free in its
Own right to deal and at the end to know
A task complete.

I overstate the case
Purely for emphasis; I know, I know
Upon what narrow ground our feet may tread,
The deaf determinants, so many cards
Dealt that we cannot alter. Yet there are
Moments at which the spirit stands and turns
And holds its place.

What is this spirit then?
Each bird that flies was hatched in humbleness
And falls back, having sung (At Höchstadt now
The ragged peewits dip and quaintly call,
And larks, like fragments of the earth flung up
To drift as motes upon the eye, sing, sing
And sing again)

The spirit also flies
And sings and falls. It is the true and fine
Embodiment and savour of the man -
The ways he came, at bidding or at none,
The way he goes, past expectation on,
Towards his total utterance. He declares
Himself and dies.

Against his spirit stand
The banners and confusion of the world.
Retreat is sure - his only victory
To wear his pride and even at the end
To live as if immortal, to grasp yet
His fragment of resolve and take it on
Clenched in his hand.

*   *   *

Joe, Mara, I've heard told
Of Persian nomads poor as mice, who seek
Pasture continually in their arid land,
Wandering with gaunt cattle to traverse
The miles they know. Each year they swim a broad
River, upon whose bank they leave behind
The sick, the old.

And calm there and bright-eyed
An old man sits, his dog in puzzlement
Crouched at his feet. Unblinkingly he hears
The bleat of goats, that climbs above the roar
Of unabating waters, and the shout
Of swimmers as they battle to attain
The further side.

His journey must end here.
He did what he could do, but now a day
Outfaces him at last. This was to come:
A contract binds him that was drawn and sealed
Before his time; its final clause rules now.
His part is to defer to it without
Complaint or tear;

And, granting this, to mark
The temper of the time and to allow
That dues are to be paid. As passion once
And labour used his strength, so now a new
And stricter task is set him, to endure
At the last outpost and without relief
Hold it till dark.

Of such, I say, is grace,
Man's truth to God; or, if you rule God out,
Truth to the cosmos built in hierarchies
Of sense and function, duty and desire,
Unfolding, yet perpetually fulfilled,
And bidding every note of being sound
Fitly in place.

* * *

The rain comes down outside.
Joe, I can see the tree you painted there,
Caged by those railings like a bird, its leaves
Trembling and shining. What I've said derives
In part, as you have guessed, from Shakespeare's
thought
Of order and propriety, but from
Much else beside -

From all I learned, or all
I chose to recollect: the tale of Christ;
Old tenets of asceticism; belief
That right would scatter wrong; philosophies,
As Plato's, only partly understood:
Eternal truths (or such they seemed), like pictures
Hung on a wall.

Eternal truths? I see
The roofs of Nürnberg streaming. It was here
That Dürer worked, and Stoss, and Wolgemut -
Cast bronze, beat gold and painted in a world
Of dark brutalities, in which a man
Might yet search out within the laws a place
To act and be.

Above those earthly laws
Paced an infallible and labouring God,
Whom in His Trinity the artist took
For teacher and exemplar. Here was truth
In its three elements - authority,
Charity, grace - here the engendering will's
Pattern and cause.

And so the plant struck root,
As the Urpflanze (Goethe's postulate),
Given sweet soil and temperate air, explored
All capabilities its genus held
Of strength and order and pursued within
The terms of its creation perfect form
Of stem and fruit.

That order lived and died.
The laws were spurned; the limits against which,
As on an anvil, the conceiving powers
Beat out their theme, were lost, and discipline
Bartered for empty play. We turned aloof
To inner chaos. Selfhood sank to mere
Assertive pride.

And yet it was not quite
Forgotten what there lacked. The heart itself
Recalls the certitude with which it moved
In pulse with something greater once, the old
Entente it had with reason, how a faith
Administered its sufferings and gave
It wrong or right.

* * *

What compass shall we find?
Mara, you talk of things I half believed
O nearly forty years ago, but now
Reject and fear. You seek another law,
Too airless to be borne and walled too close
To take reverberation from the free
Declaiming mind.

Yet, painting, you accede
To joy that strides beyond the narrow paths
Mere Politik prescribes. The way leads on
Through your own passionate, inventive soul
(That's freer and less free than you suppose)
To forms an inward force compels, to meet
An inward need.

That way, those forms, that grace,
These are your talisman - o hold them fast,
And may your turbulent and generous heart,
Under their blessing, irrigate what else
Would be Sahara; for within the self,
Set wholly to its dearest purposes,
Are source and base

Of ecstasy and power.
Mara, you shake your head and won't agree
Or be persuaded. And yet each aspires,
Surely, to hammer his equation out
And, in the face of scorn and transience,
To write his hieroglyph, before it's lost,
Upon the hour.

Or take the thing instead
By way of metaphor. Consider then
Cellini's Perseus, slim and helmeted,
Whom magic made invisible, whose arm
A patron goddess steered. Exultantly
He tramples the sprawled body and holds up
The terrible head.

And it is time that lies
Mortally struck, whose petrifying eye
Unglints and glazes now. The Perseus stands,
Shaped in erosive air but sovereign in
This faultless episode, this moment he
Has singled for unpassing, in which death,
The hunter, dies.

And as intent and skill
In Genesis one word embraced and bade
Day out of dark, divided land from sea
And seeded, greened it, peopled it, so now
Another word emerges and proclaims
New order, new conjunction, new desire,
New purpose still.

That world transfigures this
And makes its glory of our stumbling will,
For there reality accepts the act
And winnows it. The language pares to rune,
Movement to ballet; predicate disrobes
To transcendental clarity and weds
Antithesis.

But nothing is spelt out;
There's no exclusive text or disquisition,
No choice, Joe, of one statement or another,
No patient build of fragments to the sudden
Unity of an ultimate perfection;
No blazing seven-fold trumpet-call around
Our walls of doubt.

What shall I say? Each deed,
Each shape, each passion yields itself alone
In marriage to a strict regarding light
Under the dyarchy of love and mind.
O ceremony! O rule! To what divine
Centrality you gather in, to what
Enhancement lead!

For each, divested of
All sophistry and arrogance, invades
That which it is his metier to bless,
Seeks out the art and heart of it, the bright
Shadow its nature casts; and for him then
The other and the self-in-other bloom
In pristine love.

And somehow is attained -
In part, ephemerally, unsurely - that
Ground beyond time and the opacities
Of which we had no thought; an absolute,
Balancing peace and tumult, glimpsed and then
Lost, and remembered only as a point
To be regained:

Is that what Plato meant?
Mother of mothers, holding up your child,
Did you fear this, as in all innocence
He looked out from the flesh, that he should see
What distance summoned, what fierce provinces
You could not rule for him, what peak required
His lone ascent?

* * *

Patience, I've nearly done.
I assert nothing, nothing. I doubt even
What I believe, and doubt my doubts and doubt
All scaffolding one builds upon a wish.
But two things hold (let me say this, at least) -
Rocks, I suggest, for feet to ground on:
Freedom is one,

The freedom of the heart
And soul and mind; surrender that away
And honest pride is gone. The other's love.
The two are married, for how otherwise
Were truth to be accepted and forgiven,
Or the self's voyage to be other than
Failed from the start?

Rain, rain, as if to drown
All sense and nonsense; and the lights prick on.
Some bird has flown into the tree below
And perches like an emblem on the bough.
Make answer, friends; I am as much as you
In need of hope. Explain the world to me,
As night comes down -

Night, but as if a wing
Circled out there, pale-feathered against dark,
Above the traffic and the lonely tree
And the soiled parapets. O secret bird,
Be local to us still - dip, hover, glide
And soar again. Through our long winter, love,
Remain and sing.

Absent Friends - "A few went into the jaws of chance"

Absent Friends

A few went into the jaws of chance.
One for the antipodes and the end
Of his stretched lifeline's tether sailed
To seek a better friend;

And one by torchlight forded
The night of drowsing snows: a third,
Shell-struck in battle, like
Tinder blazed up and charred.

The grass treads them; and I
Fumble in December,
Clipping the spent roses. No more
Can I in truth remember

That great shout through the blood
When grief burst in; for all,
All is at two removes now
And here on the heart's wall

Only the dark likenesses hang
Of three with no renown,
Time-touched, type-cast by memory -
Introvert, cynic, clown.

Who then survives, turning
His face from the wind's fret,
Holding the winter with a ghost's passion
And weeping for it? Who yet

Fingers the abacus, counts the stairs,
Watches as the year returns,
Like an old bus up the valley bringing
Bird song and daisy-chains?

Wrong-headed Jack, with a deep
Bellyful of laughter, who ran
Like a stag once; his antlers
Tangle in the whiplash thorn:

H.P. Hart, cerebrating sadly;
Williamson in flames;
Scott, who could have been built an empire
And perhaps did so. Names,

Names - I could write down a hundred -
Blond Darby, Cockram in doubt;
S---- born middle-aged; Rimmer; Lanaway
Who bowled his heart out;

David, pressed like a leaf between
Tedious pages; Fradley there,
Licking his pencil in silence, glimpsing
Plato's forms in a chair:

And each who sculpted like a freak of weather
Feature upon that world,
All whom those nostalgic summers greened and budded
And the centrifuge hurled

Outward upon themselves, who wander
In exile past repeal.
All with that first momentum run and run and pace
The winner at their heel.

The Dead

Their dust speaks louder than victorious guns -
Who sleep, when all is said, because she was
Their lover and their land. Always she was
The statement of their inarticulate tongues.
Cloud not your eyes. Remember them with songs.

The Moment

Her gaze struck like the candour of the day
From the white, guarded bed;
It turned with kind intolerance away
The rubbed and sorry words we tried to say.
'Children die too' she said.

We saw her through the sweetness of the air
Glance past the minutes' tread.
Her eyes dwelt on the door and Death was there,
Absurd and diffident beneath her stare.
'And I shall die' she said.

Death of a Gardener

Into autumn the year strides, he weakening
Abed by the bright window. How the sun's honours,
Mauled in the last skirmish, scar and dwindle -
Poppies trailing; columbine, candytuft, cornflower
Stricken mortally: geum, stock, larkspur
Wane and spindle.

The spectrum narrows. Only his roses now
Have the stuff of fire in them - Dickson's Flame,
Pax, Virgo, ride the surges of the mist
As for a sea-burial; Mermaid, McGredy's Yellow
Spend the summer's hoard; Concerto shows like
Blood on a wrist.

He shakes his head for love for them, that hang
Sharp on the air as speech - his speech, whose whole
Craft was their husbandry - and, like utterance done,
Praise but no more belong to him who first
Wed, grafted them. He flickering, they burn
Sorrowless on.

He foundering, the stiff leaves fallen crumble
To their cobweb veins, as the spider prudently weaves
Blankets against the cold, and the hedgehog creeps
Yawning beneath his quilt. Now sadfoot past
The dripping haulms, unpausing where the poplar
Trembles and weeps,

Bat-circled she is gone, Demeter's girl,
Down for her bitter sojourn, whom the flowers
That baited and betrayed her shall restore.
Sleep-locked they muse, Fay Mark and Blarney's
Daughter,
Suzy, Trevithian, Firetail, Golden Ducat,
Agathon, Galcador.

All drowse their term - he guttering, he with hands
Gnarled on the covers. Suddenly his words
Fly up like thrushes startled from a bough.
O hills of his last land, green-throated, pass
Here under other tutelage or be
Enfranchised now.

And you, his loves, that shine through both the worlds,
Unflawed for each, in last November grant
Comfort to him - Penelope, Monique
Faithlessly tender, Ena Harkness swarthy
And best-beloved. Forsaking you it is
You he shall seek.

(For the poet's uncle)

Family Connections

When only so high, I reckoned
Uncles knew, aunts even.
Knew? Lived to a purpose, I mean;
Outstared the devils, judged
The right thing to do in a second;
Held on leash the great mastiffs -
Time, hell, heaven.

I watched them and with awe,
Trilbied ones in sheer
Knife-edged trousers, their rage
And gentleness, the hairy
Forearms, shaven chins. I saw
Their dames with them, benign - no doubt
Apparent, nor fear.

Bert I recall and him best,
Word-grudging man.
His metier was seed and leaf;
Taught me to plant, shouted at his cur
Which barked back unimpressed,
Knowing him better: taught me to dig,
Which I still can.

Liz ruled him. She sat upstairs
Cutting out dresses
On the bedroom table; came down
Stiffly - her feet were bad - to author
Pies like legends: gave herself airs
Absurdly, but her vast body uttered
The warmth which blesses.

Others come back to mind,
Though dimly, be it said:
Shy Lucy and Tine fearsome
With her bent mouth, Bert's sisters;
And what's-her-name, more refined,
With a real necklace, Fred's wife -
Ah yes, Uncle Fred....

Uncle Fred, you seemed to be
Of exceptional merit:
Gloved Sunbeam-driver, jingler of
The milled florin, nonchalant
Poser on our thin settee.
Such sweet certitude later
I would inherit.

But I didn't, and there's the truth.
The exemplars died
And the thought came, they had had
No certainties but had sidelong
Glanced at me, muttering 'Youth,
Lucky youth holds the thread.'
'Yes, youth', they had sighed.

Well, what was I to do?
Start from scratch, clearly.
I looked for signs everywhere, leafed
Famous books, pricked my ears for
Oracular voices, chased any clue:
But the pundits refuted each other
Always or nearly.

Despair becomes easy, God knows.
You can settle quite young
For a distancing from thought.
Or can you? For thought drives on
Willy-nilly and flows
Like a brook over the stones
Or drink over the tongue.

And looking into the glass
One morning you know
Obscurely of something changed,
Of this rejected, or that:
And the day and the month pass,
The year, the life; though there's nothing
Tangible to show.

Nothing tangible; and yet
It's as if you were pitted
And measured against a force
Tough and wordless inside you.
You take love, what you can get,
Body or soul's gift, the one
Vision permitted.

And there, there let it rest.
No use pretending
You're on some brink. O my dear
Remembered ones - do you sigh again? -
I learned only, as might be guessed,
That the whole business is mystery
From start to ending.

But add this, in retrospect -
It was so full of grace
And subtlety that, if it was
Devised, only a brilliant god
Could have done it. I reflect,
My friends, on the marvel of
That time and place:

The house, with earth breathing outside
And shabbiness within;
Small, homely things affirming it -
Unlocked doors, a dog scuffling,
Flagstones dark with rain till they dried,
Lincoln Creams and the teacups
Brought chattering in:

And the seedy wall-clock creaking
Testily, always wrong -
Subverting the regime, or
Trying to, that would explode
This gentle microcosm; seeking
To hold fact and dream together
As in a song.

Like a song indeed all this
Teases me still -
Written by the dead, perfect and
Not to be tinkered therefore
Into worse or better. It is
For my ear only; none other now
Hears it or will.

Cancers

Explain this courage, how they found it possible
Each day at waking to confront afresh
Death's face ubiquitous, sense the ungoverned
Blooming of the belladonna in their flesh.

It is unbelievable. I think how Allen
Drove on obstinately to order his affairs
In case and then because; and how he latterly
Went down on hands and knees to climb the stairs.

His spirit did not abdicate, nor his delicacy,
As the pain pressed home that nothing could amend.
The crisp hair, curly from his youth, was loosened,
But he joked within a hand's grasp of the end.

And George - he must have known, though they never told him,
That the seed in his head would burgeon till he died -
He too preserved the courtesies and chatted
Quite levelly as the cars went by outside.

Then, as some drug or sheer exhaustion stilled him
He'd fall to silence and our eyes would stray.
(The television flickered on a trolley;
The windows opened on an August day).

Chalk and cheese these two, you'd think; but alike
In one thing plainly, an unstumbling tact.
Resolved not to embarrass us, they spoke only
Obliquely of the Damoclean fact.

They were shy of us too, perhaps. How could we,
For all our reaching sympathy, guess their mind?
We were the undoomed, held by a thousand threads
To the trivia they made ready to leave behind.

Fear there was, and a kind of exaltation.
It was as if they had turned their look to the snows
And appraised the ascent; almost as if they'd heard,
Distant and voiced like music, a wind that rose.

Then language foundered. They could not say goodbye;
Nothing was left to declare or be debated.
They went abruptly, stepping free from their pain
Into whatever world they had created -

Kingdom or blinded void, you must judge as you will.
But it seemed to us that with unassailable grace
They glanced at the heart of our terror and rebuked it
And that darkness itself was held in their embrace.

Return to Horsham

Yes, the hill's clad in young timber now,
Chattering with birds; but that's the smallest change:
From Compton's Lane to Pondtail and the Dog,
As far as Blackbridge and the Bishopric,
Trim tarmac's spread, gemütlich houses stand,
Lamps, letter-boxes, cats and dustmen range.

Thus here homo prolificus gropes out
For Lebensraum upon the spongy fields.
Stoat, rabbit, badger, grasshopper fall back
From the rough probe of lawnmower and spade
To lick their wounds: cut off by this advance
The couch-grass fails, the nettle fights and yields.

Smug garrisons of shrub and flower march in -
The turncoat yew, the mercenary rose -
To flank the sand-fed turf. Where foxes barked
Minx, Anglia, Minor purr; where hedgehogs coughed
And moles moved alps, the brain-washed bitches whine,
The testy doctored terriers piss and nose.

What of the town we know and rooted in?
Poverty's hunted like a stag now. Some
Cramped terraces remain; but Newtown's cleared,
That nonpareil of grime. In East Parade
Garages, painted affluence; Richmond Road
Reft of its cherry-trees, the old man dumb

Who rang his bells and shouted at the birds.
Where's Ommick, selling papers? Jockey Knight
Bawling his 'Rag and bone'? And where's Tom Street,
The agile one-legged tailor, who we feared
Would brain us with his crutch? Who speaks of these?
I'll supplement his tale, who sat to write

In staider vein the record - Albery,
Loyal historian (himself at last
Caged in the theme). For how should he relate
The death of Carter, fiercely diffident,
And gentle Lucy? Or of Nellie who
Rode off in that white cloak upon the blast?

Of Tharp too, toppled like a single pine?
Him I mourn here, the bonfire of his eye
Doused in the dust, who on the angels' side
Clumsily fighting barely understood
Schoolboys and life at all, but from his tower
Looked with misgiving down as they passed by.

Gone then, but left some dint; while others yet
Still lose their way or find it. All that shrill
Hubbub of hearts he never quenched was flung
Buzzing upon the world. A few went down
Under the shout of guns; the rest move on
Across the lonely terrain of the will

Towards their truth, by purpose or default.
Fare luckily, my friends! Do you, as I,
Cartoon yourselves upon the pouching flesh?
Husband your patience: we must learn to bear
Time's aphorisms, worse than sticks and stones,
And grin like any cloth-capped stander-by.

I pause before my earliest home - stone-roofed;
Set like an old man's body, out of true.
Crooked with long arthritic damp, the walls
Lean on four centuries, as already when
They greeted me: their honour's not their age,
But the strong loves they gave their shelter to.

O she who laughed and ruled that shabby house,
Sickness and pain have touched her. He too ails,
As never once, the gardener of her days.
The year's rub goes against them. But they ask
None of your pity, who together built
A mystery that blossoms and avails

In the bleak tempting-time. She also, who
Bore her child there and on that stroke of joy
Was curtly widowed, carpentered a faith
Well keeled, well caulked, to ride her troubles out:
And clear as her calligraphy these three
Saw their vocation from the start. But I,

I failed you all, it seems. Should I have served
That god of frenzy without break and sung
Endlessly of the spirit's conflagration,
Birth into dying, voyage through the flesh;
Man finite with his charge of beast and flower,
The language of the spheres upon his tongue?

That question's rhetoric: I lacked the gift,
Though seasonally the fever ran in me
To shuffle words. One only in a host
Plays them to win - soon surely he will come,
Being due and overdue, even here perhaps
Blazes through childhood to his apogee.

Fresh folk, young timber: may the yield be good.
The boys run in from football now, and some
Are beautiful as dancers. Blind with mist,
The bell-tower rides above them as the dusk
Anoints the trampled pitches. Soon they drift,
Out of the gate and past the beeches, home.

How the leaves shine! One weeps, but not for sorrow.
O brave deciduous love, that day we went
One of our deaths devoured us. To return
Is pale ghost's work - mere standing in the wings
To brush a sleeve or catch a piteous eye's
Splinter of hope as the last light is spent.

Night grasps those boys. Which sleeps without a grief?
Which wakes and counts his chances? Now the park
Whispers with dew, as southward in the cold
Moonwhite the Arun slides to hit the race
And dash beyond the mill. Again, again,
The old clocks hail each other through the dark.

Rudolph and Loni Fuchs

It is a bitter thing,
Losing such a city;
And Prague was in their eyes -
An unyielding dignity
That forbade compassion,
A deep-troubled aloofness -
Prague, the edge of their pride,
Their look was her distress.

Two of them, that the years
Had rooted in too well
For late transplanting.
Rudolph, aging and frail;
Sad, but the Surrey wood
Drawing a boy's passion
Of lyrics from him - words,
Gentle desperation.

And Loni, deep-voiced,
With the unstartled eyes;
Touched lightly by the years
Though with their passing wise;
She, she on whom her youth
Kept still its breath and hue:
Loni. She was the most
Beautiful woman I knew.

These two. One does not win
In life so many things
To which the heart may turn
As to a peace. Time brings
Pleasure in numbered hours.
But those lamplight evenings,
The teacups cleared away,
Come in such reckonings.

For however shyly
The talk opened, it moved
Inevitably and led
To the verses we loved;
The quality of words,
The poems plain and hard,
Tender and feminine,
Read and spoken aloud.

O Rudolph! O Loni!
We were friends, were we not?
Did not those moments
When each separate heart
As such movement of words
Went like lips into a smile
Like a face into the sun
Make that avowal?

There were no years to teach us
The other's ways and will;
Only those hours there were
Of you, Rudolph, a while
Reading from Mörike
And your own poetry:
Words of Hitler's language,
Gentle incomparably.

And of you, Loni;
Dark colours in your voice,
A depth and a kindness,
A girl's ghost in your face -
Only those hours. Friendship
Stands logically on years,
Month locked into month.
For us only those hours.

And all the hours are spent.
That stubborn bitterness
Death has broken for ever.
Prague in a wilderness
Lies yet unfree. But they
Have left their grief and gone
On another exile;
And everything is done.

We shall retake the city,
Bring laughter, reunion,
To the long boulevards;
Run up the flag again.
But they are beyond joy.
Kindness is gone, the five
Senses and the passion.
Nothing is left alive.

Only the memory,
Precarious in a friend,
Soft as a ghost returns
Of the undaunted mind
In its hunger for beauty,
Its love and search for language
As a music, an edict
Of men and their courage.

You of the new Europe,
Poets in a joyous
Equal dispensation,
The doubt gone from your voice,
Consider them. Consider
Those who endured and held
When there was more darkness
Than light, when hope went cold.

Who in the uncharted
Marshland of this time
Wandered out brave-footed
To mark your safe path home;
In whose unfaltering hands
Lay inviolable things.
Guarded, kept sure for you
Through rough journeyings.

Rightly consider them,
My two friends that are dead,
Though you shall never guess
Anguish that is ended.
Unclench the four still hands
Of two that lost a city -
Take what is in them. You
Are the continuity.

M.M.H. Portrush 13.6.75

Most women are jealous, perhaps; and sons
For some biological reason
Fail to react. It was Frances at last
Who said 'She were luvly, your mother,
Yes, Bill, luvly.' You were all but eighty
Then, helpless, that June to calendar
Your last month and summer your last season.

Yes, you were a handsome woman, a damned
Handsome woman; Frances was right.
We failed you there, and I concede it;
We should have given you more admiration.
Frances, who came from Blackpool where they know
What's what, who tended you and talked to you,
Saw it at once gladly and without spite.

Famously handsome. They say my father
Catching sight of you in the street said,
Before he knew you, 'There is the woman
I'll marry and none other.' He and I
Touched only through your body, for he fell
At the steel beanfeast. You and he had barely
Time to manufacture me in bed.

But you managed it; and so I stand here
Grieving in Ireland, as the waves
Canter at the edge of this great meadow
Like fillies in the distance. Your coffin
(Quite tidy, indeed; you would have liked it)
Is fitted like the last piece of a puzzle
Into its place, the perfectly coffin-shaped grave.

'A good woman', the parson said, well-meaning.
Nonsense, I thought, she was my mother -
Unsure of herself, vain and rather snobbish,
Loving me exorbitantly to the point
That I clucked with annoyance. One does not
Grade people like cutlery or butter:
Each is himself finally and nothing other.

For yearly we spin inwards, in towards
Our target of fruition, tasked
Unwittingly to tie the circle's ends,
Until our ultimate, entire and single
Eccentricity is fully uttered,
As yours is now. O you who gave me
Allegiance unremitting and unasked,

Whose fleshly nose and hesitancy of speech
Twinned mine, whose nature mine was kin to -
Romantic, stiff - I think what else we shared:
God, Thomas Hood and heroes, miracles,
England, of course, and hope and conquering love -
Ubique gloria. Rest now. The sea
Changes to an orchestra, crashing into

Jupiter, the last movement, joy outsinging
Fragility, despair. 'Be gay,
Praise her, ha ha, she managed it after all;
Handsome, ha ha, damned handsome; to the end
She could quote old Hood, ha ha, she could smile,
And she loved, ha ha, she loved what she loved!'
She loved, and her soul flies up and away.

(For the poet's mother)

J.B. - November 1977

He sang and died
As northward the last needle swung in him:
And friends drew closer round and saw him on
Between the words and rain. He turned aside -
O streets! the day was gone, the night, o roofs!
Locked and impassable. They watched him ride

On from them now -
O desert of the city's heart! - beyond
The speech of blood to blood and past their hail,
Through upper pastures of the flesh where snow
Falls deep and deep: on a last tree some bird
Carved out in ebony upon the bough.

And music then,
Better than tears or voices, spoke and told
Quite certainly of how the will of love
Must take despair into itself, and pain;
Devour all passions, even death: the theme
Trod through the silence and was stilled again.

Against the night
Flesh glimmers faintly yet; the land is yet
Divided from the sky and lit, the tree
Clear as by glance of stars. The bird takes flight;
The bough swings back, the shadow's dark, but breast
And underwing are crimson in the light.

(For Joe Brearley, the poet's English teacher)

J.B. - 19 November 1978

Ceremonially I set
Pencil to paper. I write
Of your memory, fresh yet,
Sapling-strong: for your
Friendships I write; for her
Who soared with you into
A marriage of eagles.

We are what we become;
But the child we were
Is never exiled nor
Does our birth-land ever
Wholly yield us. You were
The clear-eyed boy always
Of those old photographs,
Agog at the world's
Talk and to-do. And Yorkshire,
Though you mocked at it,
Ruled your blood - the hills
Spurning rhetoric, stones
Script-dark, the rhythm of
Black walls running and turning.

With Yorkshire plainness
You thought, you questioned.
You wanted to understand
Everything, to enthrone gods
Or dethrone them. No kitsch -
You wanted everything
To be true and musical,
To stand on the ground
With its full weight and speak
In chime with the planets.
This could hardly be; but
It was all heroic.

And you saw each person
Quite separately, how each
In his own fashion toiled
And wrestled his devils.
Each could prosper, you thought -
The Yorkshireman's zeal
For a good bargain -
Muster his strength, then
Rig ship and sail for
Colchis, the Fleece.

So you came to live
In each of us, striding
In without knocking,
Taking the best chair,
Leading the talk. We were
Delighted, irritated, conquered.....

Dear ghost, we drink to you.

Why did you leave us?
Why did you go silent?

(For Joe Brearley, the poet's English teacher)

In Memoriam S.W.K.

Ten years ago
The grey ship moved and Plymouth slid astern.
The dockers waved. You, standing at the rail,
Dreamed the homecoming:
And at your side pressed those that would return.

Into the cage,
For the far latitudes of death you sailed,
Across the English sleeve of wrinkled sea
For that sixth continent,
Over the curving shoulder of the world.

And you were killed:
And we knew, she and I who shall meet never,
Grief like a slackened bowstring, shame in our own
Unstilled, unfaltering pulses
That you should be twenty-two years old for ever.

But you came back
To tread your lost dominion and untrace
The desolation scored upon her brow
And marvel at again
The dice-cast beauty of that stricken face.

And she, yes she
Took your young ghost one hour into her care.
In fantasy she lay within your arms,
Giving you life in death:
And now your unborn child calls from the stair.

To Boris Pasternak

Pasternak, they deny
The monsoon and the thunder,
Crowbars of grass that prise
Paving-stones asunder.

They are deaf to the count-down,
As the tall spirit aims
Its warhead of truth.
They spell out their names,

Writing history, ignorant
That the liquefying blow
Must erase them or the long
Fall-out strike them low.

Pasternak, your bones guess
What shall survive - pity
Talking to grief, all home,
Love wandering the city.

Dying

Past life now, but not dead -
A bird's flutter of breath -
Brittle as peasticks, you speak
Without consonants to death.

Give way. The very air
Denies itself at last;
Lips fumble, but the time
For parleying is past.

Yet, yet you raise an arm
In travesty of will
And aim your wounded eyes.
The dialogue runs still,

Though I, excluded, hear
Only your mumbled part,
As in pure obstinacy
You falter and restart

And mouth your desperate words
At the besieging fear.
The even voice of death,
Unheard save by your ear,

Unhurriedly deploys
Its clinching argument,
While you in wilfulness
Dissent, dissent, dissent.

After the Explosion

We scoured the room afterwards (you remember?)
And found mere fragments - two silver cups
Dented and tarnished, the dog-eared snapshot
(Some vacant youthful face), a shabby screen,
The two carved elephants wandering unfed,
Cigarette-papers, a perforated pair
Of dusty bloomers.

Leave it. You'll discover
Nothing to knit the scene again: there'll be
In the broom-cupboard no trapped buzzing word
Nor coded message in the chimney-piece.

All went in the great boom. No, surely,
No-one forestalled us, stuffing what we look for
Into a sack marked 'swag'. Nor can I credit
Berkeley was right, that a thing ceases
When the self turns away.

Be reasonable. A detonation
Rumbling for eighty years - what would survive?

Why do you search again? Why weep?

(For the poet's uncle and aunt)

W.G.D. - Missing, Presumed Killed

And no report came back at all. I, long after,
Dimly imagine you - putteed, helmeted -
Taking your stretcher out past the craters,
Cutting wire under the flares, not returning.

Each spirit is itself: gentleness may breed out
Into faintheartedness, strength into obstinacy.
But the blood's debt and derivation hold:
Our bond is there and does not ravel.

We would meet as friends now, I humbly
The elder: there would be between us
Mute graces of communion. I grieve
With the ghost of this, the deprivation.

To defer to the verities, to mime them -
None achieves more. Each with flawed allegiance
From truth fails and falls, in love as in battle.
You were as near to courage as one gets.

For to die thus was something, at the rite of
Mercy before the basilisk. If you trembled
Or were cursing, it does not matter; the act,
The mere endeavour, that suffices.

Death, o death. I see you, my father:
You stand there, sensing the hurled destruction.
Your eyes quest, timelessly; your look
Casts forward to hunt among the years.

Hear me then. Time is an expedient
And I dispense with it. I am coming now,
As death raises his fist against you:
I demand to be your last comrade.

(For the poet's father)

A German Interlude - "The mountains held out their hands"

Ballspielerin (Bronze Figure)

She stands alone,
Nameless, her voice quelled.
The pose is held.
Was the ball ever thrown?

Who saw her so
And trapped her thus? Watch still -
Perhaps she will
Turn now, and laugh, and throw.

Anteroom

The mountains held out their hands
And bade us halt here. A city
And yet not - a time rather,
Setting us at poise, that made us
Love's offer, heartbreaking and late.
Episode was it, pause between
Youth's lost Hesperides and some
Hoped trek, before declension, to
The nubile south?

Too late, perhaps. But with what
Leaping of the spirit we viewed
A fief of kings - squares, spires,
The ochre palaces that seemed
Somehow contrived, like backcloth
For a fictitious action. We
Wandered among the crowds, knowing
Most would die here, while we
Went scatheless on.

Sheraton blazed, Arabella,
And the snow drove between them.
Beyond, days of departure.
Sorrow does not enter. We
Knew this city as one knows
A book, a song, a face.

But one thought, as Aschenbach did,
Of the south - an itch, a hunger:
Trampling heat, with oranges
A mere arm's length on the bough
Away, the diamonds of the sea.
Where but there did our dead carve
The huge insignia, raise
The capitals of our being?

Who tells a life? The biographer
Snuffs an empty room, explores
The surface of an old table,
Winnows a few griefs. But we,

We were here, here. Can you make out
Clouds blushed half by the moon, half
By Munich's aura? Snow lies upon
The small rocks of Isar, caps
The Frauenkirche, there is no
Rift in it on the Wiesen;
No rift for the spring to edge
Into, nor do we wish it.
Silence serves us well, the year's
Death and nil - an unmarked page
For pencillings, a clear thought
In winter's brain of summer.
A clear thought; one wins, you see,
From the higher ground again
A further bearing on the
Hidden purlieu. But still it is
Past the horizon that the
Lines run in.

Soon we shall go,
Turn, though this past pluck at us,
From the city's crags and defiles
Over quiet Moos, out by the
Chessman churches, towards some
Arm of the taciturn sea:
South, when the moment comes - that
Day's scent, as of lime-blossom,
Drifts in sometimes on a warm
Uncertain wind.

At morning -
From how far off? - the mountains
Beckon. Are they relenting,
Or does some god of wishes
Make division in their stone
Breakers? We shall know soon.

Der Sänger

He looked down into the bottom of his glass
And sang, thinking of the love he had missed
By chance and might have had or years ago
Had read of in some book or had possessed

And heedlessly cast out. He heard the rain
Pepper the window as he paused and sighed,
And, leaning on the beer-stained table, let
The Weltschmerz swamp him like a running tide.

So he began again and spread his theme
To net the world. He sang of birth surrounded
By the grinning masks, of smooth virginity
Brought low for nothing, crisp-haired youth confounded;

Courage trampled in and forgotten: sorrow
Uncomforted for ever; cities humbled
That flew their banners, breasting the noon light
In summers once; tall columns down and crumbled.

Outside, the rain. Now flat but sostenuto
His notes beat through the talk. All turned and saw
How, spectral in the smoke, he sat alone,
Drunk or possessed. They cursed him, but with awe.

He touched on the cosmic wrong; and anger
Thickened his trembling voice and darkened his face.
His words came choking out, "The thread is broken!"
He climbed on a chair. "O God, there could be grace!

I see it, but not here - the huge guilt toppling,
Mined like a cliff! I see our sun at height
Fall like a smoky shadow on that threshold,
The champagne waters leaping with delight!"

He swayed. They took him down and led him gently
Through the glass door into the street outside.
He leant against the wall beneath the lamplight
And none was there to listen as he cried -

"O painted earth, turn from your weary passion!
Or will you shape it all again in vain?
Abate your lust!" He heard the drinkers laughing,
The muttering interminable rain.

Encounter

Stachus lights under rain
And in Hertie the modish
Posture of dummies.
What in his slurred
Jumbled Bavarian
By Strassenbau in empty
Prielmayerstrasse
He of a sudden wailed -
Blear-eyed, stubble-faced,
Swaying out of the darkness -
I had no idea, and speeded
My step to pass:
I think no
Notable pronouncement.

Flabby, unwashed;
I shrank from
Imagining how his body's
Distasteful orifices
Oozed, dribbled, stank.

And who would wish to pass
The run-down facade, enter
This brain's Rumpelkammer?
Littered it was bound to be with
Sheer kitsch and dusty
Into the bargain.
What had it learnt that
Was not worth dismissal?

But in one another somehow
We were caught up; I knew
It, wishing it other.
Identity in that sour fabric -
What focal wound or
Fistula? - had uttered,
From fear perhaps or festering
Guilt at its own lack, this
Tasteless, inherited, self-pitying,
Semi-comic ululation.
It sought
Mere human counter-sign,
Ungarnished word.

The cry
Judges me still, my passing.

The Years Pass - "What does one say when a year goes?"

New Year's Eve 1959

What does one say when the clock bestows
Its coup de grace on the year that goes,
Breaking a moment, casting a spell
On remembered time, and the bursting bell
Climbs on the air like a rambler rose?

Children sleep as a street lamp throws
Shadow on foreheads and tangled hair,
Light on the curtain's furbelows.
Listen: a creak on the empty stair -
Something passed as we laughed and rose.

Something passed as we laughed and rose.
The lamps burn on, the same wind blows -
What should have plucked our hearts as then
We turned to the dying fire again?
What does one say when a year goes?

For Christmas 1962

Moralising beast, caretaker
Of this green house, steward of the skull's
Ill-lit and draughty manor, it needs
No astrologies to read your doom.

Clearly you were blest: witness
Pity, ecstasy, all those
Deeds in the gust of morning;
Witness your old proclivities -

As, smitten, to kneel, claiming
All guilts into your stipend, from
His who at the first benison wept
To theirs, the yet unseeded;

And, on your small autonomy standing,
To proclaim love viable and carve it
On the rock-face. So now proclaim it,
Here in midwinter. Send your voice,

As the wind shouts and scathes and time
Lost on the great moor circles,
Gently into the darkness. Plead
For the arrogant and misbegotten.

Winter Scene

This is half a metaphor.
Much has died -
Leaves cobwebbed, branches brittle;
The rest
Halts in mid-stride.

You also pause, bearing
Numbly at heart
The frost of your season;
You die
Also, in part.

But waiting is the hurt.
You have got
No certainty; the earth's
Spring comes
But yours may not.

Yet you hold on, as if
To an oath
Blindly taken. You wait in
Foulness,
Impotence, sloth,

And in folly surely, for
Nothing was
Ever promised - no hope
Hinted
Nor even loss.

And you demand miracle
And the soil's cold
And the wind pushes at you
From north.
And you grow old.

January 1969

Daggers of the east wind; earth hoof-printed,
Frost-stiffened; crisp leaves of a dead season
Twitching under a sun bright and empty
As a madman's eye. I pause for no reason

But, as a god might or the fox from a bush,
To watch you walk ahead, silent between
The wind-thrashed hedges, bending as you climb
Past bramble and bryony and evergreen.

You pace on, through your thought. I can see,
Beyond you, on the ploughland a mile off,
A flock of white birds, settling and rising
And settling again, like a blown handkerchief.

I feel each step you take, feel each of us
Vicariously the other, and your youth,
My middle-age, mere variables upon
Some theme that teases and employs us both.

There are paths here I shall never thread.
One is older, being able to think of another
Which way he will go, whether he will see
More subtly and more lucidly, and whether

He will stand sometimes, as I here,
At the equipoise of two arguments,
Comprehending both, balanced between love's
Temerity and the counter-violence.

Odds are it will snow tonight, these lashed thorns kneel
To shoulder their load, and the tawny furrows
Go blindfold under stars. You turn, and as you turn
There is death somewhere, the fall of a sparrow;

The sun stares, the shadow moves out from the gate,
Frost drives to the stem's core. Somewhere
The act of love is blindly perpetrated,
As if there were hope. The gulls drift near,

Squalling now, hungering. Walk on, my blood,
Whom the unshakeable unities constrain
And the old sins admonish and the statutes.
I would not wish you to be spared this pain.

May 1977

The leaves broke late this year;
There was late frost, hail,
As if we had given
Offence somehow and were in
Some obligation of grief:
But it comes now, like a
Lost one again smiling.

And I too after deep
Winter returned, but brought
No triumphs at all, only
Older bones and a mane, yes,
Scanter than spring's.
I came
To this room again - the
Hoardings outside, the
Sounds from the street.

And there
In sun at Gräfenberg
We found them, the scattered
Ammonites, read them
Like a script written
Before thought, life's seal
Stamped in the rock.

We cannot
Think of such time, number
The wings fallen. Gods,
Do you try us, claim
Our small utmost, this
One small gift
Singing its best?

Then stamp the
Seal, joy, oh colour
The stone, fault it; that
The rock flake and show,
An aeon on, your true
And inward shape, the
Perfect whorl.

Report
Of now, of each, of
Circuits meeting; say
We were blest; and tell
Of our feet treading
These paths, our talk and
Silence, of the bees
Moving languidly
And the heart sometimes
Unable to speak;

Of the leaves breaking
Early, breaking late.

Old Man's Prayer

God that made me, see me go.
Footprints on the earth and snow,
In shop-windows as I pass
Briefly imaged in the glass,
Miniatured upon the eye
Of the glancing passer-by;
Touch of water, creak of stair,
Words upon the empty air,
Words upon the empty page.
God that made me, age by age,
See how dark with grief and lust
My spirit runs into the dust;
Love ungiven, joy untaken,
Honesty and faith forsaken -
Where's the deed that I was brought for
And the truth I should have sought for?
You that at the faring forth
Knew my little ounce of worth,
God that fashioned me, if ever
Hopes were built on my endeavour,
Give me pardon for my sin,
Call the heavy mortgage in.
With your hand undo the pain,
Cancel him you launched in vain:
God that made me, make me again.

Aneurism 1985 – “Grant us our names"

Aneurism 1985

No warning. The small noiseless bomb
Exploded in my head
And blood poured into the skull's carafe
Like Côtes du Rhône, so red.
Then darkness nursed me till I woke
Upon the hospital bed.

Knife they ordered; but flesh was yet
Untuned for such event.
Time, time must pass; and, wife, you watched
As days limped in and went.
I lay there, neatly piped and wired
Like some experiment.

Speech was difficult; meaning
Unstitched itself from word:
Sentences seemed to float on air
In gilded legend, blurred -
Script unreadable and remote,
Visible but unheard.

Once, you say, I spoke in sounds
Angled and black in tone,
Which had for your ears the smack and shape
Of language's meat and bone.
Phrases and such ran free, but alas,
Their sense remained unknown.

Was this talk from the distant past,
Through centuries unrefined?
Etruscan was it, Sanskrit or some
Pre-palaeolithic kind,
Ancestrally planted and now expelled
Out of a crevice of mind?

Probably not (though the fancy tempts).
But what was I trying to say?
Only that death was for others - perhaps
The luckless one who lay
Opposite me and was silent, too
Broken and shut to pray.

Yes, others. I had yet to list
The texts I would desire
Read at my funeral service
To warm it with their fire:
'The grass withereth, the flower fadeth' -
That thunder from Isaiah;

Job also - 'When the morning stars
Sang together'; and Donne -
'Batter my heart, three person'd God';
Shakespeare's 'heat o' the sun'
And his sonnets - I needed time to choose
How many or which one.

Music? "Du holde Kunst"; and Handel's
"Trumpet shall sound", for sure;
Watts' "Dying crimson like a robe"
Strong, on the Rockingham score;
And Haydn's "Trauer" – the Allegro, say,
From Symphony 44.

That seemed enough; my cloudy wits
Paused there and applauded.
Forgive me; this was not arrogance:
These keepsakes I had hoarded
Brought joy, even in that place; it was
That joy I now recorded.

Death is for others the world over
Today, I thought again.
Wish this, not reason; for a scene
Prepared itself, as then
The knife's turn came. I had no idea
How it went in or when

Or where it aimed. Waking, I barely
Grasped what had gone by.
Senses returned, in disorder, slowly
And separately - heaven knows why;
The circuits that had joined them were
Bruised, I guessed, or awry.

Thinking was then a trick or game -
Somewhere you had to begin.
Snapshots from childhood filtered back
And most with Horsham in:
The sloping floor at 46,
The testy mongrel, Prin;

Shops in the Carfax; and the walk
To Denne Hill and beyond;
The Arun bank, where poplars stood,
Each slender as a wand;
The forest, where my battleship
Sank in a hammer pond.

Stone-roofed and draughty 46
Time cannot yet destroy;
But wild the garden, gone the folk
That loved me as a boy.
(I make a mental wreath for them -
Herb Robert, Traveller's Joy).

And each day you were there, each day
To cheer and comprehend:
And others followed - daughter, son,
A brother and a friend -
In kindness on my halting talk
Or silence to attend.

For longer hours I sat alone,
My brain so logic-blind
Its function seemed to other parts
Of body reassigned,
That toiled in darkness but without
The dogmas of the mind.

(The mind's a zoo, where axioms,
Like tethered beasts, reside,
With labels as to source and breed
And use and such beside;
Each standing listlessly, to be
Indifferently eyed.

But I was in a wood, so still,
Wild creatures, as if tame,
Advanced to lick my outstretched hand
And watch me without blame.
They looked their truths at me before
Retreating whence they came).

A Rubicon was forded. God,
One changes without knowing!
Upon the wall the shadows change
That Plato's fire is throwing;
The climate in our blood will change
And set a fresh wind blowing.

It blew on me. I felt time run,
But not in days and hours:
Time's only clock is change, the simple
Surge and fade of powers -
The wax and wane of men and beasts,
The petal-fall of flowers.

Dim, Dryden says, as moon and stars
Is reason to the soul.
Earth fleshes us and truly we
Are agent of its whole;
Yet each may utter for himself
As on some brief parole.

("O Spirit, what in me is dark
Illumine, what is low
Raise and support") Whose words he speaks
The stammerer cannot know;
He sorts them, sings them without peace
Before he has to go.

Outside the building roses bloomed;
I saw them, white and red;
When evening came they hung like lamps.
I lay upon my bed;
The pillow was as sharp as nails
To one part of my head.

And fancies drifted round me as
I ached and tried to rest:
Truth is offered us - yes, but not
In formulae expressed;
Only the truth that truth exists
And summons to a quest.

Within the man is winnowed out
What mind and senses claim;
His centre sifts and orders it
Into symphonic frame:
And all in sum and separate
Wins consequence and name.

He works to build a truth that will
Allay his stir of need,
A part of truth that would not be
Save by his touch and heed,
Whose music only thrusts to life
Through him, as through a reed.

Fear and despair this music's voice
Soars out of and above:
He hears it from his mortal ground
Miraculously move
To absolute. It is his bid -
What prompted him? - for love.

Namer, he thus is named, whom these
Strange harmonies fulfil:
The grace and essence of the man
Arcanely they distil -
His love, for which his name is name,
His one and mystic skill.

And death is part of it, our death
(I spoke this to the air).
The night lay on us then; outside
Was darkness everywhere.
I could not see them, but I knew
The roses were still there.

A dog barked in the distance. I
Could hear a far clock chime
But lost count of the strokes it sent
To echo out and climb,
As loud then soft upon the wind
It told the so-called time.

I listened, but my body's strength
And certitude were spent:
Words buzzed about me, but I scarce
Could gather what they meant.
A gate was shut. I had no glimpse
Of where the journey went.

Did it run back, perhaps, to seek
A point at which, as when
Before the hills in order stood,
All things would stand again,
And clocks throw in their hands to go
The way of dogs and men?

I could not say. One needed faith,
Faith shuttered and resigned,
That knew no further truth could be
Discovered or defined
Until we turned from Plato's wall
To see the light behind:

Faith picturing nothing, speech nor form
Nor even shadow cast;
Faith such as holds when faith is gone
And thought of it is past:
Sheer faith that some strange love and name
Will touch us at the last.

But if the love must be forgone
Because of our love's debt,
Grant us our names, defeated though
We be and lost. O yet
Pronounce each name - a word, no more,
To utter and forget.

The clock, as if it understood,
Began to strike once more,
The dog to bark and bark again
And louder than before;
And it seemed as though the roses' scent
Came through an open door.

Name me, I said, name those I love.
I was too tired to weep:
The prayer - for such it was - within
Ran stubbornly and deep.
Name all that live and fear and die!
With that I fell asleep.

* * *

I wrote this later on. It goes
Disjointedly and ill
And looks no better on the page
Than cliché ever will.
The point is that we lived the thing
And it lives with us still.

We'll walk upon our downs again
To Druid's Grove and on,
Where oaks and beeches build their high
Untidy Parthenon,
Our feet affirming ways marked out
By others, who are gone.

A single horse will graze behind
The hedgerow of his field;
Then by a single pine we'll see
The Dorking Gap revealed;
And pausing glimpse, or think we do,
Some outcrop of the Weald.

It will be autumn - leaves ablaze,
Birds gathering to go;
Stems baring noiselessly to let
Blood-coloured berries show:
Echoes and silences, as if
A word were spoken low,

So low, we cannot hear. You'll bend
Above an inch-long mouse
That lies twig-stiff upon the earth,
To pity it; and thus
In allegory death's rite shall be
Played out in small for us.

But then the counter-sign. For turning
Almost with fear, we'll see,
As once before and yet remembered,
Emerge imperially
The genius loci from its cover -
A lone deer running free.

Gone in a trice, dark-coated and
Ungraspable - a child
Might take if for an unfleshed soul
Or symbol of the wild:
Gentle, benevolent though aloof,
Untameable but mild.

Life, spirit, purpose - on and on,
A thesis without breach:
But, though we name all in the rite
That love and impulse teach,
The metaphysics of the thing
Dance round us out of reach.

* * *

Status quo ante? No. Though I'm
Still breathing, after all.
Outside, a robin struts and fussy
Blackbirds run and call;
And through the door prospectuses
For life insurance fall.

What did I find? That to the sick
Unreckoned powers belong
And that the helpless bear us gifts
More often than the strong,
Lending their blemishes and death
For burden of our song.

What learned? We must affirm, affirm:
And blessed are the meek,
For the great affirmation comes
Most bravely from the weak,
As the small aconites we hid
Will show their heads and speak:

That truth has to be lived, since simple
Reason cannot win it;
And, as in Hamlet, there is pain
And error to begin it,
With no Euclidean chain to prove
There's all or nothing in it:

And, as with Hamlet, there's no theme
Or overt moral shown
But planes and vistas that the heart
Had never guessed or known:
And truth can touch us in the end
By metaphors alone.

'Beauty is truth' - one metaphor
We start to understand -
Ghost, presence of the absolute,
That walks on every hand.
I look out now to where the sun
Falls on the blameless land.

Nothing is uttered, but it seems
There clambers on the air
The jubilate of a psalm,
The whisper of a prayer;
And it's as though some small and strange
Epiphany were there.

I think - the old god calleth all
By name, the scriptures say.
Believe or not. But who could shake
His head and turn away?
Name us, I murmur, as you named
Our fathers yesterday,

If so you did.
                    The world outside
Is spread before my eye.
The trees stand in their kingdoms still:
Birds range in squadron by:
The sun is curtained: striding clouds
Rule distantly the sky.

Envoi - "Diamond shivers on it"

Envoi

Diamond shivers on it; time's weather
I have looked and seen my level's
Absolute now, a semper erit

(This fragment of verse was found
under the poet's pillow after his death.)

PIGEON GROUNDE

Pat Earnshaw

Gorse Publications

British Library Cataloguing-in-Publication Data

A catalogue record for this book is available from the British Library

ISBN 0 9524113 3 4

Printed by Antony Rowe Ltd, Chippenham, Wiltshire.

Typeset by Alastair Thompson, Paris, France

for Gorse Publications, P O Box 214,
Shamley Green, Guildford GU5 0SW,
England

Cover illustration by Shirley Veater (Tel: 01273 306 003)